CW00643252

Secrets of Dog-Training

By the same author

Sight Hounds, Longdogs and Lurchers

SECRETS OF DOG-TRAINING

D. Brian Plummer

ROBINSON PUBLISHING
London

Robinson Publishing
11 Shepherd House
Shepherd Street
London W1Y 7LD

First published by Robinson Publishing 1992

A copy of the British Library Cataloguing in Publication Data is available from the British Library.

ISBN 1 85487 119 6
Typeset by Hewer Text Composition Services, Edinburgh
Printed and bound in Great Britain by the Bath Press, Avon

I dedicate this book to Bert Knight,
a *savant* from Dornoch who once uttered
the cryptic epigram: 'Commonsense
ain't that common, is it?'

Contents

Introduction

Watching people has always been a source of great pleasure to me, long before Desmond Morris afforded the general public a Rosetta stone with which to interpret man's peculiar mannerisms and gestures. I've sat and watched people for hours until I've become aware that I am almost a different species or to be more truthful, I rather hope that I am a slightly different species, for from what I've observed I conclude that man is a muddled-thinking creature and possibly one of the most illogical species ever to grace the face of the planet.

I've just spent a morning sitting in my van, parked in a supermarket car park in Thurso – population 8,000 (and unlikely to exceed that number) – and I don't consider the time I spent there was wasted for I have learned much. My observations have been disturbed by the incessant barking of a cur-like dog, the sort one sees in any Middle Eastern town, chained to the railing of the supermarket, which has barked without ceasing for an hour or so, its repetitive staccato chant infuriating the householders who live nearby.

A lady, Dalmatian on leash, has just passed the car at something between a rapid walk and a canter – the velocity of her movements determined by the dog that is towing her around the town. Her right arm has probably developed to proportions that would make Arnold Schwarzenegger envious, but I appreciate that she must dread her jaunts around town with her spotted ward. On the way to Thurso I saw a collie dog, brought north by tourists that, excited by its new-found freedom, had finally found an outlet for its latent herding instincts and was running a local flock of Cheviot sheep to a state of exhaustion before its breathless owner had caught the beast and cajoled, and probably bribed the irate shepherd to silence. The collie is now tied to the caravan at the site near Dunnet Beach exhilarated by its exercise perhaps, but bewildered by the beating its owner has administered in the hope that such chastisement will correct the dog's behaviour. The chances are that once free of its lead it will resume chasing of sheep and cause its owner such anxiety and grief that he will return south to suburbia with a suntan and a myocardiac infarction.

My reverie about how the herding instinct is so closely related to hunting – the two qualities separated only by an element of restraint – is broken by the sight of a short-legged mongrelised Jack Russell-type terrier that, free of its leash, has chased a terrified cat under a V registered Volkswagen and is baying furiously at its foe, oblivious to its owner's pleas, commands and entreaties.

The general public is slightly antipathetic to dogs and all things canine for that matter, and I cannot but sympathise. Newspaper and television are peppered with interviews with victims of the attentions of pitbull terriers and rottweilers and no doubt a scientist with a Ph.D in mind has published an emotive article indicating that the earth samples he has collected in certain parks contained, in addition to silica mineral salts and a high level of humus, a goodly sprinkling of roundworm eggs (passed via the faeces of dogs) which will, once hatched, grow into larvae which could produce an unpleasant disease known as visceral larval mygrans that causes blindness in young children and susceptible adults. *Avant garde* extremists predict an Asimov-type world in which all pets are forbidden, following hot on the heels of AD 2000. Frankly, I have every sympathy with such people. Dogs can often be pests that give little pleasure to their owners and a great deal of anxiety and anguish to those who live adjacent to them.

Yet it is perfectly simple to train dogs to an acceptable level of obedience and prevent them from becoming a nuisance to neighbours and stock-keepers alike. It is also a pleasure to own a well-trained and obedient dog; and to the school of thought that states that dogs too have a right to express their emotions, give vent to their instinctive desires in any manner they think fit – even if their actions irritate others or cause concern or anxiety to the community in which these dog-owners live – I offer this book!

1

Facts the Breed Books Don't Mention

To choose a dog simply because of its aesthetic appeal is a mistake, though frankly most dogs are bought simply because the owner 'liked the look of the breed'. It is also a mistake to purchase a dog simply because the dog is pleasing to look at and the breed book concerned states that that particular dog is the *beau ideal* of what a dog should be. Authors who write breed books are usually devotees of a particular breed and hence can see no fault in that particular breed. So devoted are these writers to the breed of their choice that to them at least the breed is sane, sensible, reliable, intelligent and so versatile as to be able to play the mandolin and fill in its owner's tax returns.

I have yet to read any breed book that states 'This dog is unintelligent, recalcitrant and almost impossible to discipline.' Yet many breeds of dog are virtually impossible to control off the lead in a public place. The self-same breed may perform well in the confines of the demonstration ring and even win the coveted CD (Companion Dog) award, but free of the restrictions of the leash, free of the confinement of a ring of spectators, that dog will often run amok, refuse to return to hand and be a positive nightmare to own.

It is also unwise to approach an exhibitor, with an armful of dogs on a leash, at a major Kennel Club show and heed his or her advice about the disposition of the breed he or she is showing. The chances are that the exhibitor is besotted by the breed and blind to the faults of the dogs he or she owns. It is also extremely likely that the exhibitor, despite the fact that the dog is shown in pristine condition, will not have the slightest idea of how to train the dog or to even control the animal off the leash in a public place. This obviously isn't true of each and every exhibitor, as the number of show champion dogs that have won obedience awards attests. However, the majority of exhibitors seen at dog shows often have less than total control of their wards.

How, therefore, should a person who is attracted by the look of a particular breed go about finding out its character. A visit to an obedience-training class may well allow someone interested in some of the more commonly seen breeds of dog to study the nature of the breed type. Yet again it should be pointed out that dogs that perform well and appear very obedient while on a leash or restricted by a crowd of spectators may perform less well in conditions of total freedom. Professional dog-trainers can also be consulted about the nature and tractability of certain breeds they may have had occasion to train. However, just as a Formula 1 racing driver may not be the person to consult about driving the family car in urban conditions, so also the professional dog-trainer may be able to achieve results with slightly difficult breeds of dog that would sorely tax the abilities of the amateur.

Personally, if I was interested in obtaining an unusual breed of dog to keep as a pet, or to share my home, I would seek out the advice of someone who had also kept such a breed as a pet, and perhaps even attempted to attain rudimentary obedience with the dog. For instance, I keep and breed a rough and ready strain of working bearded collie – a rare type that is kept and worked by shepherds north of Inverness. I find the Polski owezarek nizinny or Polish lowland sheepdog (similar in appearance to the working bearded collie) particularly attractive, but before I considered purchasing one of these hirsute herding dogs I would seek out a sensible and sane person who actually kept a specimen of the breed as a house pet and ask the following questions:

Is your dog easy to control?

Does he return to hand readily when he is running free?

How does he behave with children or livestock?

What sort of relationship do you have with the dog – is it docile, biddable, trainable, etc?

I would then seek out yet another owner of the Polish sheepdog and ask the same questions. If I received similar favourable replies I might consider buying such a dog. It can be argued that the majority of dog-breeders start out as pet-keepers and might be equally qualified to express an opinion on the desirability of the particular breed; it can also be said, however, that once a breeder acquires an interest in a particular type of dog, he or she becomes oblivious to its personality defects. In short, I would ask a motorist who owned a Lada about the performance of the car and not consult the sales representative from the local Lada showroom.

Make no bones about it, the perfect breed of dog, *sans* physical or mental defects, has yet to be born. As I write this book, the Plummer terrier – my life's work – is awaiting recognition by the Kennel Club. Any breeder of the type would be only too willing to tell a potential buyer that the breed was a composite of bull terrier, fell terrier, Jack Russell and beagle. Few breeders would be prepared to tell a customer that these terriers are wilful and spiteful with other dogs and difficult to kennel if they are not worked regularly: if I may quote one of my mother's Russian Jewish proverbs – 'No fishmonger advertises his wares as stinking fish.'

Thus the aesthetic appeal of a particular breed of dog may attract a future dog-owner, but its personality traits must be considered before the would-be owner rushes out to buy a specimen. For instance, I find the Siberian husky one of the most attractive breeds I have ever encountered. They are alert, lively and usually excellent-tempered dogs where people are concerned. Having said that they have the well-earned reputation of being among the worst stock-worriers in dogdom, and are usually hell with sheep, chickens and cats. Of course they can, with difficulty, be broken of sheep-worrying, but it is the devil's own job to do so. Furthermore, while I know of one or two who live on quite amicable terms with the house cat, I know of many more that have grown up with the house cat and one day decided to end the relationship. It is also very difficult to get them to respond to recall training, and as I live smack bang in the middle of sheep country the ownership of such a dog would induce yet another coronary, so I would refrain from buying a Siberian husky – though I confess I have a sneaking liking for the type.

In fact most Spitz-type dogs – Arctic breeds with tails neatly curled over their backs – have a reputation for being quite difficult to control and, if given the opportunity, of being bad stock-worriers. This fact should be noted by anyone who is considering owning a malemute, an ostiak, an Eskimo dog or a Siberian husky. Male malemutes are often so ferocious with other male dogs that dog sled owners who use these rather slow but extraordinarily strong sled dogs to haul goods in Alaska castrate the males in the team to prevent ghastly fights. It is argued that civilisation has taken some of the edge off these beautiful and powerful Arctic sled dogs, but it is unlikely that a mere hundred years of breeding would have eradicated characteristics that have taken millenia to evolve. As an aside, the malemute may well be the most powerful haulage dog on earth – the famous Bear Paw Lobo once pulled a double-decker bus along a street and could snap the inch-thick sisal ropes that tethered it by lunging against them.

Yet one seldom encounters a breed book that does not eulogise the qualities and beauty of the Spitz breeds, but even more seldom does a breed book tell of the personality problems one is likely to encounter. However, Spitz are not the only breeds that are difficult to control and are certainly not the only breeds that first-dog-buyers should consider carefully before purchasing.

Scent hounds are far from being the most biddable of dogs and are certainly not suitable animals for those who require a pet to return instantly to hand. Scent hounds – staghounds, otter hounds fox hounds, harriers and beagles, and the once very popular Hush puppy dog, the basset – have one aim in mind: to pursue the scents of sundry animals and to run head down on those scents – oblivious to the cries of their owners. Of course such dogs can be controlled – a trip to a local beagle or basset meet will allow the potential buyer to see the 'whips' (an unfortunate term perhaps) controlling an entire pack of these hounds – but there must be a great many owners of beagles or bassets who would not consider owning another scent hound of any breed again.

Personally, I like beagles and because of their excellent noses I incorporated them in the Plummer terrier mix, but a tale will certainly illustrate my point regarding the disobedience of the breed type. When I taught in Rotherham I exercised my terrier pack in a woodland in Herringthorpe where the small number of rabbits that lived in the woods provided enough scent to entertain my terriers, which sought out but seldom managed to catch the fleeing conies. One Saturday in October I encountered a middle-aged, mud-bespattered lady lying face down on a fallen tree sobbing piteously and muttering 'Benny, Benny'. At first I suspected the lady had been molested, and being a somewhat timid man who is reluctant to seek out problems to add to an already overburdened lifestyle, I approached cautiously, for I had heard of rather sickening tales of damsels in distress and the unfortunate fates of knight errants who had endeavoured to help them.

Benny it transpired, however, was not an attacker but a male beagle she had decided to exercise in the woods and which had disappeared as soon as he hit the trail of a rabbit. He had struck the trail on the Friday morning previous to the day I encountered the lady and she had spent the night searching for him. I abandoned my hunt and helped search for Benny and a matter of two hours later I found him four feet deep in an old badger set baying at a rabbit that had run to ground in a gallery adjoining the set.

At the risk of a bad pun there is a 'sting in the tale', so to speak. As I helped the muddy and dishevelled lady to her Mini parked on the edge of the wood, I noticed her rear window boasted two stickers which read 'Be owned by a beagle' and 'Once one has owned a beagle one wants no other dog' – a sentiment I believe the lady must have endorsed.

It is only fair to add that despite a scent hound's natural disposition to explore scents regardless of the pleas and entreaties of its owners to return to hand, it would be difficult to find more placid, gentle-natured family pets. In *Tarka the Otter* Henry Williamson affords his anti-hero Deadlock a sense of almost Gothic foreboding for in Deadlock's veins ran the blood of the Talbot hound dogs which had supposedly eaten man. Yet the staghound (Deadlock was a staghound not an otter hound) like all its relatives invariably has what is referred to as a 'sunny disposition', though at one time Talbot hounds (the ancestors of most modern British scent hounds) were the most feared hounds in medieval Britain, and in Carson Ritchie's opinion almost altered the course of British history.

Mark Anthony's speech in Shakespeare's *Julius Caesar* concludes with the rabble-rousing yell of 'Cry havoc and let slip the dogs of war'. The majority of books concerned with the history of breeds of dog state that these dogs of war were a type of mastiff similar to the American pit bull terrier. In fact, there is conclusive proof that five hundred fighting mastiffs accompanied Henry VIII on his military campaign against Charles V of France, and that on the Spanish campaign English mastiffs not only destroyed the Spanish infantry but attacked the dogs used by the Spanish army. However it is more likely that Shakespeare's dogs of war were scent hounds used to track down Caesar's assassins; and in that capacity Talbot hounds were greatly feared.

During the wars between Scotland and England opportunists with a bent for training dogs often stood back from the main affray and used Talbot hounds to hunt down vanquished or wounded knights endeavouring to escape the field of battle. Cumberland specialised in producing hounds for such purposes partly because of its geographical position and partly because of the natural disposition of its natives to exploit the scenting ability of hounds – trailhounds, John Peel's pack, etc.

These scent hounds displayed no animosity towards the people they tracked down – when they came on their prey they usually greeted them by barking joyfully. To these man-hunters, the pursuit of man was a game, albeit one often played for the highest possible stakes, but there is no indication that they ever tried to attack the men they were pursuing.

When the famous man-hunter John of Lorn set out to capture the vanquished Robert the Bruce he disdained to borrow Kendal-bred hounds and used hounds bred and fed by Robert himself – which pursued the trail of their master joyfully in the hope of being reunited with him. Legend has it that the Bruce recaptured the hounds and escaped into the mists of the Lowlands, though other tales give a more painful conclusion and state that the Bruce was forced to slay his beloved hounds to escape capture.

Had the Bruce been captured – and his trial and subsequent execution would have been a matter of course – the Stuarts would never have come to the English throne, the British Civil War might never have taken place and in all probability the USA might still have been a part of the British Empire, since porphyria, the debilitating malaise that sapped the energy of George III is attributed to a gene carried by Robert the Bruce.

This brings us to the breeds that do not usually greet strangers quite as cordially as did the Talbot hounds, namely the greeds that are commonly used as guard dogs – German shepherd dogs, rottweilers and dobermanns.

Now, such are the peculiarities of the British and British laws that while a dog may be used to deter an intruder, the self-same dog is not permitted to maul the intruder should he attempt to gain access to one's premises. There is a story of a burglar who sued a householder whose bull terrier attacked him while he was ransacking the house. Such are the peculiarities of British justice and the audacity of the

British criminal. In short, a guard dog is permitted to scare off an intruder but not to savage or hurt him.

So what exactly are the qualities that scare off an intruder? For, from time to time one sees mongrel dogs bearing little or no resemblance to any known breed running on chains to guard scrap yards. Now some of these dogs are amongst the most ferocious animals I've ever encountered – and their ferocity is accentuated by the fact that they are restrained by a chain – which I'll explain later. Yet they do not frighten a would-be intruder as much as a more tranquil German shepherd dog or a dobermann or rottweiler.

It is the reputation that a breed has for ferocity that deters a trespasser, and some breeds acquire reputations for ferocity in curious ways. Many breed books state that the deterrent value of the German shepherd dog results from its similarity in size and shape to the palearctic wolf – and thus the appearance of the dog awakens race memories in man, for pre-Promethean man supposedly had an instinctive fear of wolves. The similarity of the wolf to the German shepherd dog is remarked on by Strebel in his celebrated work *Die Deutchen Hund* (*The German Dog*). He tells the story of how, at the Dresden dog show, some borzois that had come from the famous Perchino Kennels in Russia and had been used by the Archduke Nicolas Nicolasovitch to hunt palearctic wolves, went berserk when the German shepherd dog Phylax von Eulau I paraded before them. Strebel concludes the Borzois mistook the German shepherd dog for a wolf. In fact, no one who has ever seen wolves and German shepherd dogs could confuse the two, for wolves bear only a superficial resemblance to primitive German shepherd dogs. It is highly unlikely that man has an inherent fear of wolves, anyway. Lopez's *Of Wolves and Men* thoroughly explored the subject of wolf attacks on man and concluded that there was no instance of a healthy wolf attacking a man, woman or child on record. Rabid wolves will attack human beings, so for that matter will rabid cats, but Lopez concludes that the legendary devourers of men such as Corto, the wolf that held Paris to ransom in 1407, and the awesome Beasts of

Gevaudan that supposedly slew 64 people from 1764–67 were dog/wolf hybrids and not wolves – but the subject of exotic hybrids will be explored at a later date.

In all probability the reputation the German shepherd dog acquired as a truly formidable guard dog is simply due to the fact that the majority of the world's police forces use it for crowd control and man work; but it is its amazing perspicacity and versatility, not its ferocity that makes the animal such a useful police dog.

The reputations of dobermanns and rottweilers have been acquired in a different manner; and the publicity these breeds have achieved via book, film and TV has had disastrous results, as the spate of hideous tales of rottweiler attacks from 1987–90 attest. These attacks, followed by an even more furious spate of attacks by pit bull terriers, have made the British public intensely suspicious of large, aggressive-looking breeds – and prompted Parliament to legislate the fate of breeds of dog that have acquired a certain notoriety.

Alistair Maclean in his bestselling book *The Last Frontier* unwillingly gave dobermann breeders a financial shot in the arm that attracted totally unsuitable buyers to purchase dobermanns. In the tale the hero, a James Bond-like figure, is treed by Eastern Bloc police dogs and contemplates doing battle with his trackers. However, once he realises that the dogs pursuing him are not German shepherd dogs but dobermanns the hero promptly throws in the towel, for while he believes he can easily despatch a German shepherd dog he knows he is woefully overmatched by a dobermann. Maclean, who is an excellent writer, obviously knew little about dogs!

However, the publicity afforded the dobermann by Maclean was as nothing compared to the Ira Levin book *The Boys From Brazil* and the film of the same name. At the end of the film an elderly Nazi played by Gregory Peck attempts to shape the life of a Hitler clone by removing the boy's adopted father. The youthful clone retaliates by encouraging his four dobermanns to dismember Peck and the scene is not only superbly directed but horrific. In point of fact, the dobermanns used were simply encouraged to attempt to retrieve the collars of Peck's jacket and the gore and screams were added to the film later. Peck remarked that the only fears he experienced were that he would laugh when the dogs began to lick his face.

Hot on the heels of *The Boys From Brazil* came the famous 'Rosebud' incident featured in the Colombo TV detective series. An ingenious student of human and canine behaviour devises a method of killing his wife's lover and trains a pair of dobermanns (made yet more ferocious in appearance by their cropped ears) to kill when the word 'Rosebud' is uttered. Now the word 'Rosebud' is seldom used in day-to-day conversation so the dogs are placidity itself until the fateful word is uttered. The psychologist, played by Nicol Williamson, lures his victim to the house and from the safety of a health farm phones to ask his victim the name of the sled used in the film *Citizen Kane* (for the would-be victim and his would-be killer are film buffs). The victim replies 'Rosebud,' and as the dobermanns are in the same room the result is both predictable and singularly bloody.

After every showing of the Rosebud sequence and *The Boys from Brazil* dobermann breeders experience a sales boost, for the most unsuitable customers imaginable seek out dobermann puppies for all the wrong reasons.

A curious interplay between dog and man now takes place and the results of this interplay are often terrifying. Dogs are gregarious and stratification takes place among pack animals – a 'know thy place' pecking order – that produces alpha beta to epsilon category animals in stratifications as rigid as the Feudal System. If a dog is to enter the family so to speak it must enter the family at the epsilon level and be subservient to the youngest child in the family. However the type of client that endeavours to buy a dobermann puppy after watching the Rosebud incident and *The Boys from Brazil* is, to quote P.G. Wodehouse, 'a curious sort of cove' by any standards. In fact the majority of men seeking to buy a dog to emulate the feats of the dogs of Nicol Williamson or the youthful Hitler clone are not only disturbed but are odds-on favourites for being an epsilon member of the social group to which they belong. The purchase of a large fierce dog of the type described is in fact the man's rather ill-advised attempt at elevating himself to a somewhat higher position in his social group ('Gosh – look at that man with that fierce-looking dobermann').

Thus an epsilon category man who is possibly socially or mentally inadequate buys a large powerful and often dominant animal. In all probability such a man might manage to establish a relationship with a bitch puppy, for bitches are seldom as dominant as males and are usually more willing to accept a somewhat lower position in the family hierarchy (most attacks on people by large and fierce canines are carried out by dogs and not bitches). However, bitches are seldom as large or impressive as males and to the men buying a dobermann for the reasons described 'image' is all important. Thus the most dominant dog often becomes matched with the most subservient or inadequate man (and once again I have been deliberately sexist for women seldom choose dogs for the reasons just described).

The scene is now set for a plot that is as predictable as a Sophoclean tragedy – and the outcome is often as unpleasant as anything dreamed up by a Greek tragedian. Either the dog will become so dominant as to rule the house and attempt to extend its reign of terror to the neighbourhood or the owner will attempt to subdue the beast by cruelty rather than firmness and the dog will erupt or become a very disturbed animal indeed. Worse still, the really inadequate owner might attempt to emulate the feats of Nicol Williamson or the youthful Hitler clone and it takes very little training to encourage even a rather docile dog to attack a man (Konrad Most's *Dog Training*).

The reader may believe I have exaggerated the results of the interplay between a rather weak man and a potentially dominant dog. More to the point, the reader may well believe that I have exaggerated the impact such films have on the weak-willed and susceptible dog buyer. To those who believe this I say that enquiries for dobermann puppies increase when the films just mentioned have been shown, but when a showing of the *Dobermann Gang* (a film where cleverly trained dobermanns are taught to rob a bank) is given a TV viewing, dobermann breeders receive fewer enquiries for puppies despite the fact that the film illustrates just how versatile the dobermann really is.

Likewise the rottweiler that shot to popularity after the showing of the film *The Omen* in 1977. In the film a rottweiler bitch adopts the role of guardian to the devil child, Damien Thorne, and when Robert Thorne, the child's father, attempts to kill the demon, the dog attacks him furiously. The part of Robert Thorne is played by Gregory Peck – a man singularly prone to attacks by large dogs, so it appears.

Yet despite the bad publicity, the German shepherd dog, the dobermann and particularly the rottweiler are usually not only versatile and easily trained but temperamentally sound and in the hands of sane-thinking owners with some knowledge of dog behaviour and training methods these animals are delights to own. Conversely in the hands of people with little knowledge of dog behaviour or men who are socially inadequate the dogs can become devils incarnate – as the TV newsreels of 1990 depict all too graphically.

The reputation of the American pit bull terrier is to say the least baffling – though the spate of attacks by these dogs on men, women and children in 1991 caused the British government to legislate to deter the public from keeping this breed and allied dogs such as the toza – a large Japanese dog bred exclusively for pit-fighting. Admittedly the American pit bull terrier is a furious fighting dog when it engages a dog of any breed in combat, but prior to the 1990s instances of these dogs attacking people were so rare as to be practically unknown. In fact Ed Reid, a British authority on the breed, mentions in his book that it is extremely difficult to goad a Pit bull terrier into attacking a person and obtaining a Shutzhund (guard dog) award in Germany. Richard F. Stratton, in *The World of The American Pit Bull Terrier*, 1983, goes to some pains to show how reliable these dogs are with young children. Yet later in the 1980s there was considerable publicity after a Pit bull terrier not only attacked a man in the USA but actually inflicted such a mauling that the man died. Man-fighters – dogs which showed antipathy to people – were seldom used for breeding by the dog-fighters who kept these Pit bull terriers, yet somehow the same problem began to manifest itself in Britain in the late 1980s and early 1990s. What caused the appearance of these dogs is debatable. Ed Reid believes that the random rogue specimens that have created mayhem on human victims are still extremely rare. Certain anonymous dog psychologists quoted by the national papers state that these rogues are now far from uncommon. Many believe the breed has always shown a natural propensity to attack people though only recently has the lunatic fringe decided to exploit this quality and deliberately encourage or allow the breed licence to attack human beings. In all probability a combination of breeding from stock that showed an antipathy to people and a somewhat demented element of society deciding to exploit these qualities has produced the terrible injuries that seemed to be reported almost daily during the early days of 1991.

However, whether or not American pit bull terriers show an antipathy to people or not, the breed is a ferocious dog-fighter and should never be placed in a position where it can gain access to another dog of either sex. There are numerous instances of dogs attacking and killing bitches and of bitches wreaking similar havoc on the males, so it is often far from safe to allow the family Pit bull terrier to enjoy a romp or game with a dog of either sex. Some Pit bull terriers have a sunny disposition, but others are far from being sociable beasts. Many working terrier shows that cater for terriers and lurchers alike will not allow bull terrier breeds on the showground and seldom stage classes for these dogs.

Such is the nature of the breed and such are the fighting qualities that have been developed over eight or nine hundred years, that should one of these dogs tumble another dog and secure a suitable grip on its luckless victim, it requires expert skills to make the dog release its grip – and the grip is truly awesome. Pit bull owners often carry a set of specially designed implements to enable them to prize open the jaws of their dogs and allow their victim (and the word victim is an accurate one for no other breed of dog can endure the onslaught of an American pit bull terrier) to escape.

While it has to be admitted that the American pit bull terrier is a truly magnificent animal, and some specimens of the breed are not particularly aggressive, the ownership of such a dog is fraught with dangers. A Pit bull might play amiably with another dog for a year or so and never display the slightest aggression. One day an incident that is so insignificant as to pass unnoticed by the owner of either dog, will cause offence and the placid, genial animal the Pit bull once was metamorphoses into a furious attacker, hell-bent on attacking and killing its playmate. The ferocity of the first attack of a Pit bull will surprise anyone who is not *au fait* with the behaviour of these unique canine gladiators and inbuilt instinctive techniques of disposing of an opponent are manifested immediately a battle takes place. Henceforth, such a dog can never be allowed to encounter its one-time playmate, for Pit bulls separated from their victims display an implacable hatred for their albeit reluctant opponents ever after. Once this propensity to fight has been manifested, and it needs little encouragement to persuade a Pit bull terrier to attack another, then ever after the dog is unsafe with any other dog.

I must confess that when I see an American Pit bull terrier exercising free of the restrictions of its lead, I catch up with my own dogs and take them elsewhere to exercise. I am simply not prepared to risk an encounter with such an animal, despite the assurances that are invariably offered by the owners of such dogs. My actions are due to the fact that despite my admiration for the shape and tenacity of these dogs, I have made a lengthy study of the history and disposition of the breed and to say I am decidedly wary of American pit bull terriers is an understatement. Despite the fact that I have seen many delightful Pit bull terriers that were totally trustworthy with children, their propensity to fight other dogs makes them less than desirable pets for the typical family.

The Staffordshire bull terrier is possibly the ancestor of the American Pit bull Terrier or at least one of the ancestors of the breed, for the Pit bull is a taller, racier type of dog than the Stafford. Dyed-in-the-wool devotees of the Stafford are wont to say that those who breed Staffords for exhibition have bred much of the fire out of the breed, for the majority of the Staffords seen today are a far cry from the furious fighting dogs that were bred in the Black Country. That the modern Stafford is not as aggressive as its forbears pre-World War 2 is patently true, and long may this amelioration continue. Dogs that are prone to attack, fight and frequently kill other dogs are an absolute pest and far from a delight to own. During the time I taught in the middle of Staffordshire bull terrier breeding country – and I taught for nearly twenty years in Walsall – I made an elaborate study of the breed type and the owners who kept these fighting dogs. The ownership of the early Staffords must have been a perfect nightmare. Dr Roger Mugford, the present authority on the modification of dog behaviour, points out that once a bull terrier has experienced the joys of combat it is virtually impossible to rehabilitate the dog and the animal becomes a liability to own. It becomes impossible to exercise the dog off the leash and the appearance of another dog of either sex will trigger off a ferocious outburst from the bull terrier. Walsall is the most colourful town in Europe and no place on earth can match the Black Countryman's gift for wit or the coining of epigrams. The saying 'To own a fighting dog, one must be a fighting man' originated here and while the saying has now taken on a machismo meaning that only the tough and loutish are capable of controlling bull terriers, the original meaning of the cliché was quite different. A pit dog caused such havoc with other breeds that the whole neighbourhood was antipathetic to its owner and sought retribution.

Likewise the English bull terrier is thought by many to be a refined, more elegant version of the common stock that spawned both the American Pit bull terrier and the Stafford. Like all bull terriers or allied breeds, the English bull terrier should never be allowed to engage an opponent.

English bull terriers are seldom as fiery or aggressive as either Staffords or Pit bulls but nevertheless are able to give an awesome account of themselves in a conflict with another dog and are the devil's own job to extricate from a fight. Many bull terriers of all breeds are reluctant to cause trouble with other dogs, but any potential dog owner who considers the purchase of a bull terrier for a pet should also consider the problems the ownership of a dog with such a heritage might bring.

In passing, it is interesting to note that many bull breeds undergo a transformation if their movements are restricted by a chain. It is said that many dogs become intensely territorial if they are chained – and show a tendency to attack or warn off intruders who come within reach of this chain. In no breed is the guarding instinct accentuated by a chain more apparent than in the bull breeds. The most ferocious property-guarding dogs I have ever encountered were in fact not German shepherd dogs, rottweilers or dobermanns, but bull mastiffs that had been chained near the objects they were intended to protect. I have observed bull mastiffs that were absolutely delightful animals to own, become transformed when chained up. It would be interesting to investigate what causes this very rapid metamorphosis in the breed type. Perhaps the effect of the chain awakens some archaic race memory in them, for the ancestor of the bull breeds was a type of broad-headed mastiff type dog referred to as the 'ban dog' (banded or chained dog).

However, while bull breeds might be reasonably expected to display some anti-social habits, it is also fair to say that some of the most apparently placid and docile breeds can in certain circumstances become unmitigated nuisances. Some years ago, a spate of sheep-worrying throughout Britain caused me to research the subject of which breeds were more liable to chase and harm farm livestock and during the survey I had to balance the results against the popularity of particular breeds. Mongrel dogs, dogs of no specific breeding, were the most common stock-worriers, simply because mongrel dogs of no specific breeding are the most commonly seen dogs running free of restraint in the streets of British villages. Likewise German shepherd dogs were fairly common stock-worriers, because at that time the German shepherd dog was possibly the most popular dog in Britain and because there were more German shepherd dogs than any other breed, it was likely that there were more instances of German shepherd dogs worrying stock. Similarly, rogue collies, compulsive herders that were unable to switch off the herding mechanism and continued to round up sheep until they died of exhaustion or attempted to escape from the group and had therefore invited the dog to bite them by their reluctance to be gathered, caused havoc. However, no breed has such access to sheep as does a collie, so this fact too was taken into consideration during my survey. What transpired from my investigation was a peculiarly high incidence of Dalmatians and Irish setters being involved in sheep-worrying incidents – and both breeds are seldom sufficiently popular to justify this high incidence of sheep-worrying.

It must also be pointed out that the unusually high incidence of lurchers (greyhound composites) worrying sheep could also be explained fairly easily by the incredible popularity of the lurcher in the mid-1970s and the fact that poachers are apt to abandon their dogs when surprised by landowners or gamekeepers. Such dogs, left to their own devices, often endeavour to fend for themselves for several days – scavenging, catching and eating lagomorphs and rodents – but all too readily turn to stock-worrying. During the early 1970s the incredible tale of the Beast of Watten (a small village in Caithness) resulted in much newspaper copy. Flocks of sheep had been torn to pieces during a night's havoc and thousands of pounds' worth of stock was killed in a matter of weeks. Stories of gigantic black cats seen in Sutherland, the most sparsely populated area in Europe, attracted hordes of newspapermen to the Highlands in the hope of obtaining a 'scoop' of an unusual native, but as soon as the newspapermen arrived the carnage stopped abruptly. However, just as these southern journalists were about to relegate the Beast of Watten to the status of the Loch Ness Monster, the slaughter started again and armies of crofters beat the nearby forestry plantations while a helicopter carrying a police marksman hovered overhead.

Eventually the hunt for the Beast of Watten reached its climax as a 27-inch, smooth-coated lurcher was driven into open country and killed by a single shot from the police marksman's rifle. The killings ceased as abruptly as they began and the tale should illustrate how important it is for the dog owner to keep his or her dog under control in the countryside. My survey unearthed the disturbing fact that some of the least likely breeds can degenerate into savage sheep-worriers. The sight of fleeing sheep is a tremendously exciting one to every household pet, I'm afraid.

However, the tale of the Beast of Watten brings us quite neatly to the subject of that most enigmatic of breed types – the sight hounds. Without any question these must be some of the most difficult breeds to train to any degree of obedience. Sight hound is a collective name for breeds that prefer to hunt by sight rather than seeking out the quarry by searching for the scent left by a particular species of mammal or bird. The term sight hound includes the Irish wolfhound, the Scottish deerhound, the borzoi (a Russian wolf-hunting hound), the greyhound, the whippet, the Afghan hound, the saluki, the rather rare sloughi and those two Mediterranean enigmas, the pharaoh hound and the Ibizan hound – two breeds that not only hunt by sight but have highly developed olfactory senses which can prove additional problems to the pet keeper who does not wish to hunt his dogs.

Sight hounds usually respond to commands with infuriating slowness despite the fact that when they so choose they can galvanise into action with an astonishing and often quite terrifying speed. The Celtic branch of the sight hound family – the Irish wolfhound, the Scottish deerhound, the greyhound and that diminutive greyhound known as the whippet, are slightly more responsive to command than the Middle Eastern sight hounds, the Afghan hound, the saluki and the sloughi, which are not only extremely difficult dogs to train, but suffer mentally if denied a lot of human companionship. The neurotic behaviour early coursing enthusiasts attributed to the saluki, which may behave moderately well some days and on other days ignore the pleas of its owner, is often attributed to the fact that the saluki reacts strangely to changes in weight – a heavy dog, a pound or so above its ideal weight, may behave quite differently when it is coursed at its optimum weight. However it is equally likely that the behaviour problems of a saluki may well be due to psychological upsets undetected by the owner. It is a sad fact that while the saluki (and indeed the saluki hybrid – the saluki longdog) is the stock-in-trade of the down-market unregistered dog dealer, no breed of dog suffers more mental turmoil when it experiences repeated changes of home.

All Middle Eastern greyhound types are singularly resistant to formal conventional training and while they may appear moderately obedient within the ring of spectators at an obedience event, in a field where moving objects animate or inanimate may attract their attention the same Middle Eastern greyhound may well decide to ignore the commands of its owner. Salukis have a reputation for coming to hand only when they are ready to do so. Afghan hounds have an even more unenviable reputation for disobedience, and during my stint at Lichfield I experienced an extraordinary encounter with a pair of these hirsute and glamorous hounds.

Shortly after I became resident of Lichfield a breathless, almost speechless, couple arrived at my cottage and asked me whether I had seen a pair of Afghan hounds they owned. They had, so they explained, bought a puppy and been so enamoured of the appearance of the whelp that they had returned some six months later and approached the breeder to buy the litter brother of their puppy. Theirs was a heinous mistake for they were woefully inadequate about the training of the original whelp. When one Afghan was joined by the second matters worsened tenfold and the pair found they were unable to recall either sapling hound to hand. Walks with the hounds on leashes were obligatory as the pair if unexercised chewed the furniture and carpets to pieces, but neither hound could be let off the lead.

Eventually the couple built a wooden kennel in their council house garden and incarcerated the hounds in a shed with a small run built of chain-linked fencing. Afghan hounds however are some of the most athletic animals of dogdom and the six-feet-high fencing proved no obstacle to them. Time after time they scaled the wire and needed to be taken back to their kennels. Finally the young couple decided to put a top on the kennel to prevent the young hounds escaping. The Afghan saplings then set to with a vengeance, chewed their way through their kennel wall and escaped, and once running free in the fields near Whittington, they refused to come to hand. To cut a very long and rather unpleasant tale short I finally trapped one in a net I had fitted across a gateway and grabbed the other one when it came to investigate the cacophony caused by the hound trapped in the folds of the net. Lest the reader thinks this method of catching a dog is cruel and that I am indeed a heartless creature for trapping the dog, it should be pointed out that at that time, there were flocks of sheep in the field in which the hounds cavorted.

Both the saluki and the Afghan hound societies sponsor breed rescue societies and those who run these rescue societies are to be praised, for 'their cup runneth over'. These exotic, elegant and incredibly beautiful greyhounds all too frequently attract the wrong type of owner like a magnet. Breeders are remiss if they neglect to mention to their clients that a sight hound of any sort is an extremely difficult breed to train. These breeders are also being a little unfair to the puppies they are producing if they do not deter unsuitable potential clients from buying exotic sight hound puppies and adults.

Ibizan hounds and their closely related pharaoh hounds are also quite difficult dogs to train. Not only do these hounds possess the rather remote disposition of the typical Middle Eastern sight hound, but they also have excellent olfactory senses and a tendency to run head down on the scent of game. These qualities combine to produce a dog that is doubly difficult to get to come to hand in places where the scent of game abounds – and this quality of 'dealfing out the owner' – the dog acts as though it has not heard the handler's commands and continues to hunt up the trail of the animal it is hunting – is infuriating to anyone who expects rapid responses from his dog. In the hands of an experienced and competent trainer, the pharaoh hound and the Ibizan hound can be versatile and useful hunting dogs – in Malta and the Balearic Islands they occupy the same role as the lurcher in Britain – though they are infinitely more difficult to train. In the wrong hands – and anyone seeking to buy an exotic breed of dog in order to own something out of the ordinary will invariably be 'the wrong hands' – these Mediterranean-type hounds become nightmarish creatures to own and during the time when I specialised in training recalcitrant sight hounds, owners of Ibizan and pharaoh hounds were the most frequent clients.

No sight hound or sight-hound hybrid (hence a longdog) should ever be taken to places where it may encounter game or livestock until it is well and truly trained and comes to hand quickly and without question. Once such an animal has experienced the joys of the chase, it becomes extremely difficult to obedience-train or to get the animal to come to hand quickly. I have great admiration for anyone who willingly takes on an adult Mediterranean-type sight hound, or a sight hound of any type, for that matter, that has been allowed to run riot without experiencing any obedience training. I have even more admiration for anyone who can make a success out of obedience-training such an animal – and I have yet to meet a person who has made a success out of retraining a recalcitrant Mediterranean-type hound.

By now the reader must surely be wondering whether there is any breed of dog that is easily trained and yet a joy to own, so once more I must allow the reader to rummage in the bottom of Pandora's box and state that there are many breeds that are relatively easy to train and offer the owner a great deal of satisfaction both in their ownership and training.

In his masterly book *Man Meets Dog*, Konrad Lorenz divides dogdom into two distinct categories – the Lupine type descended from the palearctic wolf and the jackal-blooded dogs descended from *canis aureus*, the golden jackal. Lupine types – and Lorenz refers to the Spitz-type dogs as being typical of Lupine type – are usually very difficult to train and are prone to be stubborn and recalcitrant. Dogs descended from the golden jackal, and Lorenz believes the German shepherd dog to be the most typical of jackal-blooded dogs, are far more tractable and easy to train and while I believe Lorenz is very wrong about his classification of breed types, I would advise any person buying a first dog to purchase one of the breeds Lorenz believes to be descended from the golden jackal: the collies, the German shepherd dogs, retrievers, spaniels and allied breeds – though it should be pointed out that these breeds too have their peculiarities.

It would be a difficult task to find a more biddable and versatile breed than the border collie. True, the collies were originally bred to herd sheep, but there are few tasks at which collies cannot excel. In Sutherland a red and white strain of border collie is renowned for its retrieving instinct as well as its skill at herding and several have been used to retrieve buoy ropes to the small boats that fish for crabs and lobster along the Northern coast. Several of the strain will retrieve shot game as dextrously as would a retriever. Other collies have been trained as guide dogs for the blind or 'hearing dogs' for the deaf. Many collies are used by Customs officials as sniffer dogs, dogs that can detect the presence of drugs or nitrate-based explosives in luggage, while mountain rescue squads and teams searching for survivors amongst the rubble of fallen buildings have found collies ideal for finding trapped victims. At one time German shepherd dogs were the inevitable winners of competitive obedience and agility tests, but in the last decade or so the border collie has swept all before it in such competitions. There seems very little that it is impossible to teach this versatile breed of dog to do.

Bearded collies are a slightly different kettle of fish and may be divided into two distinct categories, the more hirsute exhibition-type bearded collies, and the 'scruffy dog' working bearded collie now seldom seen even on the remote crofts of Sutherland and the Grampians where the breed was once popular. The KC-bred bearded collie has a justly earned reputation for being somewhat scatty, unintelligent and rather difficult to train – though it is an exceedingly attractive-looking breed of dog. In *The Heritage of the Dog* Colonel David Hancock describes the exhibition-bred bearded collies as 'the dog the Kennel Club has ruined in the shortest period of time' and there is some truth in Hancock's derision of the breed.

Working-strain bearded collies are a different matter however and though until a matter of five or so years ago the working bearded collie was an endangered breed that did not seem likely to survive into the twenty-first century, the breed is making a comeback both as a working dog and as an obedience and agility competition animal. Working bearded collies competed on the TV show *Super Dogs* – though the commentator, not *au fait* with the working type of bearded collie, continued to refer to them as cross-bred bearded collies throughout the programme. There are several reasons for the revival of the working bearded collie as a working dog, not the least being that many shepherds believe that the modern border collie has been 'softened' by sheepdog trials until most strains seem fit only to 'herd five sheep on a Saturday afternoon'. While this is a gross exaggeration, there is some considerable evidence to suggest that the more aggressive style the bearded collie adopts while herding is becoming appreciated by many southern shepherds who keep large flocks of sheep.

Some strains of collie are however, in the words of Brian Vesey-Fitzgerald, 'difficult to live with'. Some strains unless given regular legitimate work are prone to be slightly hyperactive or manifest excessive zeal at herding. Some become distraught when they find human beings or animals are not huddled together in a group and many collies tend to herd or gather up their owners while being exercised. Some collies often become notorious car-chasers and need to be restrained as soon as the slightest indication of this irritating and dangerous habit manifests itself.

Certain working bearded collies have a reputation for being difficult to lead-train or tend to dislike being taken out on the lead. This is a minor inconvenience however and while the initial lead-training process might be a shade annoying there are virtually no dogs that cannot be lead-trained if the trainer approaches the training process carefully and gives the initial lead-training a little thought. According to one sporting newspaper, the working beardie often has its spirit broken by the act of lead-breaking. As a breeder of the type I believe that this theory is simply unsubstantiated bunkum and should be disregarded.

Vying with the border collie for the title of the most versatile breed of dog is the German shepherd dog which despite its large size and supposedly fierce disposition, is one of the most easily trained breeds of dog. The original role of the German shepherd dog was however rather different from that of the British border collie. Continental shepherd dogs were required in addition to herding and moving flocks, to deter large predators such as boars, bears and wolves from attacking the flocks. Hence many continental herding dogs are larger and more powerfully built than their British equivalents, for large predators have been rare in Britain since the eleventh century.

The versatility of the German shepherd dog makes it a fascinating animal to own or to train, though the epigram 'the German shepherd dog is either the best or the worst of dogs' is also very true. In the right hands the German shepherd dog is a delightful animal to train, but if untrained, allowed to run riot and not to know its place in the family's social structure, it is not a desirable animal to own or to train.

There seem to be few tasks the German shepherd dog cannot be taught to perform. The majority of police forces throughout the world and most security firms use German shepherd dogs in preference to any other breed. The breed has slowly fallen out of favour as a guide dog for the blind for the more phlegmatic Labrador retriever, the golden retriever and hybrids between the two breeds are now commonly used. However, hearing dogs (dogs used to aid the severely deaf) are frequently selected from German shepherd dog litters.

Several German shepherd dog breeders still attempt to maintain the herding instincts of the breed – indeed in

Germany the dog is still used to drive and herd sheep and cattle. To compare the herding instincts of the German shepherd dog with those of the border and bearded collies would be unfair, but many German shepherd dogs show a marked inclination to round up sheep and cattle and perform these tasks satisfactorily.

Other enthusiasts have worked the breed with the gun, using it in the capacity of a retriever or a spaniel, and the German shepherd dog often shows a great prowess at hunting up a variety of quarry. Cynologists believe the herding instinct – the driving of sheep or cattle back to the handler – to be simply a sublimated form of hunting instinct. The herding dog is actually driving the quarry towards its handler so that the handler (who has now taken on the role of a pack alpha member, can dispatch the prey. As the behaviourist Spencer expresses the action so succinctly, 'in the herding motion the blow is simply stopped short'. This is not a useless piece of data hurled in to entertain the reader, but a warning that if left to run riot or to wander out of control in the countryside any dog with a strong herding instinct becomes a desperately dangerous creature as far as livestock is concerned. Should two or more dogs be allowed to wander abroad, a pack situation is likely to be created and the pack immediately polarises into hunting or driving dogs and catch or kill dogs. Should one of the pack be a dog that manifests a strong herding instinct, the pack becomes very efficient and many times more destructive to livestock. It is most unwise to allow German shepherd dogs or for that matter any breed of dog to wander in the countryside anyway.

Despite its exceedingly powerful build, the German shepherd dog (if physically sound – and the subject will be discussed later) is an incredibly agile dog and capable of not only a great turn of speed but also of scaling apparently impossibly high hurdles. Mrs Griffin, whose prefix Crumstone was once commonly found in the pedigrees of many post-war German shepherd dogs, records that her rather gaunt, untypical male shepherd dog, Crumstone Danko, scrabble-jumped 16ft. 4ins.

Should a German Shepherd dog show an inclination to take readily to water – and some admittedly show an aversion to paddling out of their depth unless carefully encouraged to do so – the animal can be put to great use. Polly, the white shepherd bitch that founded my strain, was in addition to being one of the most versatile animals I have ever owned (she once reared an orphan Duroc piglet which became so imprinted that it accepted elementary obedience training in the manner of a dog) who hunted, worked with ferrets, hauled a peat sled and herded, was an incredibly enthusiastic water dog. She swam out and grabbed creel ropes that were situated in rock pools into which it was extremely dangerous to take a boat. This is a relatively easy skill to teach any dog that shows a desire to swim and it is an extremely useful task for a creeler or fisherman to teach any powerfully built dog.

Before discussing some of the problems that can beset this remarkable breed of dog it might be of interest to explain why the German shepherd dog was once referred to as the Alsatian – or dog of Alsace. During World War I such was the antipathy of the British to anything connected with Germany that a spate of dachshund poisonings occurred and many delightful little dogs, whose only Teutonic connection was the fact their remote ancestors once hunted badgers in Germany, died as a result of absurd and misplaced patriotism. Breeders of German shepherd dogs were therefore obliged to refer to their dogs as Alsatians – dogs of Alsace, a province with scant connections with the breed type. Truly, if the first casualty of war is the truth, the second must be those with emotional disturbances coupled with patriotic leanings.

However, just as every Garden of Eden seems to house an obligatory snake, it should be pointed out that the German shepherd dog too has its share of problems. My own strain of white or cream German shepherd dogs (white or cream is not a favoured colour amongst the German shepherd dog show fraternity and many breeders will vehemently deny they have ever bred animals of this colour) was plagued with hip dysplasia, a hereditary disorder in which the hip cavity is not deep enough to house the head of the femur, that cripples even quite young dogs. It was a great tragedy, for my strain was extremely docile and tractable and I had difficulty finding suitable outcross blood to breed out this abnormality. Still more upsetting was the fact that few other breeders were prepared to admit that they too had bred dysplastic puppies, despite the fact that at that time the malady was the scourge of the German shepherd dog. Such is the curious snobbery that besets dogdom or rather dog breeders that when I found a kennel of black and tan German shepherd dogs which were apparently free of the disorder, I was told that the breeder would not allow her coloured dog to serve white bitches and I was obliged to seek out a dog the lady had bred to mate into my very worthwhile strain. However, all is not well that does not end well. The outcross brought in a hyperactive quality that made the puppies I bred less docile, perhaps no less tractable, but certainly not as pleasurable to live with or to train.

This prejudice against white German shepherd dogs is actually quite interesting and certain dog-training manuals advise trainers of guard and attack dogs (there is a difference) not to take white shepherd dogs for training. There is certainly a great deal of evidence to suggest that the darker or wolf-grey animals have a greater deterrent value than white dogs. Yet white German shepherd dogs can and do appear in litters from coloured parents and are neither physically or temperamentally inferior to their darker brethren.

To return to the subject of inherent defects however, epilepsy – a 'fitting disorder' that seldom manifests itself before the dog is two years of age – was also a scourge of some families of German shepherd dogs (my own strain was fortunately free of this distressing disorder) but in recent years thanks to the efforts of the German shepherd dog Club the incidence of these disorders is decreasing.

The German shepherd dog is a relatively easy dog to train and displays a great willingness to learn. Instinctively recalcitrant animals are a rarity and the majority of the over-boisterous, badly mannered, aggressive German shepherd dogs one encounters from time to time are the result of mistraining and bad handling rather than bad breeding. An adult German shepherd dog is usually very much a one-man dog and while puppies readily accept a change of human owner, adults usually take a considerable time to settle into new environments. When such a dog is swapped, sold on or subjected to the treatment meted out by the typical unlicensed dog dealer, the animal becomes insecure and then manifests behaviour problems that are certainly not typical of a well-reared, healthy specimen. A properly-reared, well-socialised German shepherd dog puppy subjected to a sensible training programme by a responsible dog owner is seldom a problem to own or train – and once more it is well to heed the cliché, 'a German shepherd dog is either the best of dogs – or the worst of dogs'.

Labradors and retrievers, such as flat-coated retrievers and golden retrievers, are also relatively easy dogs to train and the majority of them are rather submissive and display a great desire to please their owners. Puppies from all retrieving breeds are usually great fun dogs that are versatile, easily broken to livestock (and the importance of breaking to livestock will be dealt with presently) and invariably display a great love of water. Anyone wishing to own a dog that will give a great deal of entertainment would do well to consider one of the retrievers.

However, like all hunting dogs, retrievers were bred to fetch shot game to hand – the breed delights in running head down on exciting scents – and in case the reader imagines his exercise ground is free of the scent of game it should be pointed out that the majority of gundogs find the scent of lark as exciting as that of grouse, partridge or pheasant. Hence before a retriever puppy is taken to country where it is likely to encounter exciting scents, it is wise to subject it to a fairly stringent training programme so that the dog returns to hand immediately it is called. The majority of the half-crazed gundogs that ruin a day's shooting and disrupt and dismay 'guns' and beaters alike are simply animals that have been allowed to hunt up the scent of game before they received their basic obedience training.

Labradors are not free of faults, however – though they are usually delightful animals to own and train. Their reputation for gluttony and subsequent obesity may well accentuate any tendency the breed has to hip dysplasia – and this problem is far from unknown amongst Labradors. Eye defects such as progressive retinal atrophy – an inherited abnormality that brings about premature blindness – are also not unknown in Labradors. Serious breeders of Labrador retrievers are however taking steps to eradicate these problems.

Golden retrievers too have their problems though, possibly because the golden retriever is a lighter-framed animal than the Labrador, hip dysplasia seems far less common in the breed. Some strains of golden retriever produce epileptics, though once again the breed clubs are in the process of eradicating this disorder.

It is difficult to generalise, but golden retrievers usually take longer to mature than do Labradors and remain skittish and infantile longer than most other retrievers. In passing it is worth noting that while the golden retriever is descended from certain strains of British spaniel, the Labrador probably shares a common origin with the bulkier Newfoundland (which possibly because of its size is even more prone to hip dysplasia than the Labrador retriever).

Labradors tend to show more of a tendency to guard persons or property than do most other retrievers. Indeed at one time the Metropolitan Police used Labrador retrievers as police dogs. Retrievers however seldom inspire the same fear amongst miscreants as a dark-coloured German shepherd dog and because of this and other problems the police now use more conventional dogs such as German shepherd dogs. It is however a mistake to consider the Labrador as a dog that will rarely show hostility to unwelcome strangers – some are fiercely protective of both property and persons. Yet despite this I would not hesitate to recommend a Labrador to anyone who was setting out to buy an easily trained first dog that would be fun to own and simplicity itself to train.

For some reason toy breeds of dogs, while often beset with physical abnormalities, are seldom recalcitrant or difficult to train. Perhaps two thousand or so years of close contact with women and children has acted as a selection programme that has effectively eradicated vicious or recalcitrant qualities in these breeds. Circuses or the now increasingly rare music hall acts do not use toy breeds simply because of their appealing appearance. Many of these toy breeds, particularly poodles, are extremely easy dogs to train and can be taught to perform the most intricate of tasks. The TV stunt dog Pippa, a mixture of various toy breeds, clearly indicates how well these longdogs can be trained and just how versatile they can be in the hands of competent dog-trainers.

Terriers, despite their small size, are sometimes far from easy to control. In addition to the fact that most terriers still retain a strong inclination to hunt any type of animal or bird whose scent crosses their paths, the majority are particularly eager to take offence from another dog. The reputation many terrier breeds have for snappiness – hostility towards human beings, particularly children – I believe is not due to genetic peculiarities but due to their very strong hunting instinct being denied or thwarted. Terriers that are worked regularly – hunted to fox or rat or rabbit (it is illegal to hunt otter or badger in Britain) will seldom display aggression towards humans. However, terriers do need a great deal of exercise to sublimate their working instincts and it is also well for owners of any breeds of terriers (other than that great terrier, the Airedale) to know that terriers show a marked propensity to follow game into holes, and they need no encouragement to develop the instinct.

Ralph Hodgson, a quite famous pit rescue expert, was once much in demand to dig out terriers which had been put to ground to seek out foxes or badgers and had become trapped in the bowels of the earth. His skill at 'fixing' a roof of a dig thereby preventing the earth falling in on the diggers made his services invaluable in Durham and Northumberland. However, Ralph was most frequently called out to rescue a pair of West Highland white terriers kept as pets by a Durham lady who was decidedly anti-hunting. Her dogs were unaware of the antipathy their owner manifested towards the sport and as soon as they were set free of the leashes ran head down on the scent of rabbit or fox and disappeared underground. Twice Ralph dug for a full sixteen hours to rescue these terriers only to find that yet once more they had 'gone to earth' the very next day. Eventually the pair went missing and Ralph assumed they went to ground, dug onto a rabbit and were suffocated by the earth thrown behind them by their digging. Most terriers, Airedales excepted, will run to ground and cause their owners a certain degree of anxiety by their exploitation of their natural instincts – the very word, terrier, means earth dog.

It is, however, virtually impossible to describe the peculiarities of every breed of dog, but the would-be owner would do well to explore the physical and mental peculiarities of a breed rather than select a certain breed of dog simply because of its attractive shape, colour or coat. Breed books are usually written by breed enthusiasts, who are invariably totally blind to the eccentricities of their beloved breeds and few exhibitors who are authorities on the standard of excellence of their particular breed are also competent trainers. Many breed clubs finance and aid auxiliary rescue societies to house specimens of the breed that have been sold to unsuitable owners and the lot of these dogs (and one supposes the lot of their previous owners) has usually been far from happy. To chose a dog purely and simply because of its aesthetic appeal is a very short-sighted policy indeed.

2

On the Subject of Mongrels

Now if all the hogwash written about the virtues of mongrels over pure-bred purpose-bred dogs was laid end to end it would encircle the earth many times over. Mongrels are always more appealing, more intelligent, more hardy, more loyal, more biddable than pure-bred dogs – and let me begin this chapter by saying that these evaluations of these canine dolly mixtures are simply bunkum.

Mongrels, according to my *Webster's Dictionary*, are 'dogs of mixed or uncertain breeds' – and I hope to explore the term 'uncertain' more fully at a later stage in this chapter – and can vary in size from, to quote again, 'as small as a flea to as large as a cow' (*Mick, an Irish Terrier*). The mental peculiarities manifested by these cross-breds are also unknown qualities – unless the owner knows the exact breed make-up of a particular hybrid. Few owners of mongrel dogs know the origins of their wards though man's vanity is such that umbrella terms readily seem to be coined to describe doubtful cross-breds. I have yet to find the owner of a large or medium-sized mongrel who does not proclaim their ward to be an Alsatian/Labrador hybrid. Likewise a lurcher owner with rough or broken-coated, fleet of foot dog on leash will invariably describe the hybrid as a deerhound/greyhound. Such is the breed snobbery that invades every nook and cranny of the dog-keeper's world that no canine mish-mash can ever be allowed to be labelled 'pedigree unknown' by a proud owner. Curiously nowhere in the world is this breed snobbery more prevalent than amongst the British and the Americans – two of the most mongrelised races on the face of the planet.

Let's deal with Webster's reference to a mongrel being simply a dog of mixed breeding before exploring the possible problems of owning a dog of uncertain origin. Some very fine animals can be bred by the deliberate hybridising of two distinct breeds of dog. The most popular mongrel at the time of writing is of course the lurcher, a hybrid of a greyhound and some other breed such as a collie or a breed of terrier deliberately created to produce a dog that is fleet of foot and with the nose and intelligence that is usually lacking in pure-bred sight hounds. Lurchers which are designed to be all-round hunting dogs, engineered to catch rabbits and hares and to procure the odd partridge or pheasant, are usually deliberately bred. Such hybrids are often excellent companion dogs, though their tendency to stray to spots where they are unwelcome (or so their owners are wont to offer as a defence in courts of law) can be a shade disconcerting.

Droppers, hybrids between setters and pointers, have been praised amongst sportsmen for their versatility for centuries and matings between Labradors and setters or pointers to produce hybrids that hunt, point and retrieve were at one time not unknown in the field of game shooting. Today, however, such cross-breds are seldom encountered and rarely bred, for pure-bred hunt, point and retrieve breeds such as German short-haired pointers, weimeraners, vizlas and other versatile Continental breeds of gundog are more than capable of fulfilling the role once occupied by these cross-breds.

Strange and curious deliberate cross-breeds are often excellent at specific tasks. The most curious one that comes readily to mind is the targhee hound – a deliberately bred hybrid between an Irish setter and a staghound and this strange cross-breed once defeated all comers when it was raced against conventionally bred sled dogs in the sled dog races that are so popular in America. To date the hybrid has yet to be produced in Britain, for sled dog racing or the use of dogs for hauling freight, occupies one of those shadowy areas of British justice – and we'll deal with this subject presently.

However, let us now return to the 'uncertain breeding' aspect of Webster's definition of a mongrel or more to the point let me present the reader with a hideous chimera that could be created by unintentional hybridising of totally unsuitable types. Let us assume that an American Pit bull terrier escapes and instead of seeking other dogs to rend asunder encounters a Siberian husky bitch who is unable to find sheep to attack and dismember but is in such a state of season that the Pit bull terrier is amorous rather than aggressive with her. The result of such a union would be too horrible to contemplate both in physical appearance and in mental attitude for the hybrid might possess the blind ferocity of the Pit bull terrier and the stock-worrying recalcitrant nature of its husky dam. Let us assume that the breeder of this litter succeeds in giving the hybrid puppies to various associates against whom he has a grudge and a female from such a union comes in season, escapes (as indeed Siberian husky hybrids will be all too prone to do) and after failing to find stock to worry or other dogs to slay is served by a passing saluki that has also escaped and failed to find cats to chase or sheep to destroy. I am acutely aware that puppies from this second mating would be too horrid to contemplate and in the words of Sheffield comedian, Tony Capstick, 'two of these could easily rule the world'. On second thoughts, for Siberian husky read Alaskan malemute and the second generation hybrid becomes more nightmarish still as it possibly has aggression, a tendency to create mayhem amongst stock and the recalcitrant disposition of its saluki sire. I have of course allowed the worst possible alloy to be mixed – a possible canine fiend to be conceived, but to those who blindly state that mongrels are a better bet than pure-bred dogs – and to writers from Mark Twain to Buchan who extol the virtues of pedigree-unknown canines, I say: 'Take on and endeavour to train such a mixture, live with such a beast or, horror of horrors, allow such a fiend to run free of restraint for an hour or so and then reflect on the wisdom of that glib statement "Mongrels are better prospects to own than pure-bred dogs"'.

It was once stated that hybrids, mongrels, call them what you will, are more resistant to disease than pure-bred dogs and in 1948 when a particularly virulent form of distemper known as hard pad swept Britain and countless valuable dogs were slain by the epidemic, many street curs survived the outbreak of the disease (many did not, one should add). This argument might be countered by the fact that when parvo virus reared its head in 1980, mongrel and pure-bred puppies alike bit the dust – though rottweilers and dobermanns seemed to suffer most from the ravages of the virus for some reason that has yet to be explained. Today it is possible to vaccinate dogs against these apocalyptic horsemen, parvo virus, distemper, hepatitis and leptospirosis – so the much-debated subject of hybrid vigour and the supposed disease resistance of mongrels assumes less importance.

It would be impossible to leave the subject of mongrels or intentionally created hybrids without reference to the subject of the wolf-dog hybrids that furnished TV cameramen with an incredible footage of film in 1990 and allowed journalists to write totally inaccurate and grisly tales in January of that year.

The cause of the furore – and no other word could describe the turmoil the appearance of these hybrids caused – was one Kenny Dalgleish (no relation to the football star and club manager of the same name). Dalgleish is a man of furious energy, enormous personal charm and a total disregard for conventional rules and regulations he considers may hinder or impede the life he wishes to live. Dalgleish had worked as a shepherd, a horse dealer and a farm contractor, and in the mid-1980s he had approached me to buy two German shepherd dog puppies to run against border collies in sheep dog trials! A heretic amongst livestock keepers, he succeeded in winning prizes at very minor events – once more his success rate was exaggerated by the press – but Dalgleish's future experiments were to cause more interest, if interest is the correct word to describe the reaction that was to follow.

In the early days of 1987 Dalgleish contacted an American breeder and subsequently imported a malemute x wolf hybrid and then a bitch of similar breeding. This was reported perhaps a shade inaccurately in the newspapers. Within days Kenny received anonymous, vindictive letters suggesting that in addition to allowing his 'wolves to tear out his throat' he performed feats that were biologically dangerous not to say illegal and sexually impossible. The hybrids however proved docile though totally impossible to train; a photographer from a national newspaper visited Kenny's kennels and photographed the bitch cleaning a newborn lamb, but these photographs were never used for they were not sensational enough to stimulate a blood-crazed readership.

Dalgleish was then approached by irate farmers who envisaged sheep and cattle torn asunder by the hybrids and also by an hysterical woman who had a child that insisted on dressing in a red cape (shades of Grimm) and pleaded that Kenny keep his wolves away from her child. Finally dog fighters (owners of Pit bull terriers) phoned him to request he test the mettle of their dogs on his 'wolves'. However, like the red-robed child in the fairy story, Dalgleish was not out of the woods by a long way.

In 1990 he mated his wolf hybrids to a German shepherd dog male and produced a litter of lupine quadroons (I can think of no better expression to define these hybrids). The doggy periodicals went into overdrive. The dog-breeding world is choc-a-bloc with rather silly people who take themselves far too seriously and when it became known that I had bred the sire of the litter, I was approached by an enraged woman who insisted that I write an article denying that German shepherd dogs in general were wolf-blooded. Now this is curious as many early German shepherd dog breeders, Strebel etc, went to some pains to try to prove that the breed had 'wolf genes'.

A puppy from this dog x wolf x dog union was sold to a woman in central London and when it became known that the lady owned this reserved and placid mongrel wolf-dog she became the victim of furious abuse and dead foxes were hurled into her garden – what the gesture was meant to indicate is still unknown.

At the time of writing these wolf x dog hybrids are still a subject of great interest to those who have a passion for owning the exotic or the unusual but frankly these hybrids usually make far from suitable pets. In the early 1980s I traced the development of the litter bred by Raymond Graham-Jones at his zoo in Southam near Leamington Spa and far from being the ravening beasts of Gothic legend I discovered that wolf-hybrids were in fact so nervous as to be virtually untrainable. This opinion is not borne out by others however for the Sigethy brothers who breed film wolves by mating wolves to grey German shepherd dog bitches think otherwise. Both brothers state that they enter the compound, where their hybrids are kept, with great caution for the cross-breeds are extremely dangerous.

I make no excuse for including the tale of Kenny Dalgleish in a book of this nature. As legislation regarding the ownership of dogs becomes more restrictive and more Draconian, men who are perverse creatures deliberately seek to keep exotic animals as a mute protest against pointless and restrictive laws. Thus wolf hybrids find a ready market amongst such people. I shall leave the subject of wolves' hybrids and indeed the subject of cross-bred dogs with a warning note.

At the time of writing there is great public concern about the ownership of dangerous dogs – to further antagonise a rather hostile public is irresponsible and to say the least a shade unwise.

3

Dogs in Literature and Legend

What exactly does the average pet-owner need to know in order to train his family dog or, more to the point, what should that owner know about the way his or her dog thinks, and how can he or she make use of this knowledge to train the dog?

First, the would-be trainer should forget all knowledge he has acquired of the dog from legend or novel. In fact, considering the wealth of information concerning dogs available in both literature and legend it is not surprising that most dogs are not only ill-trained, but their mental make-up is totally misunderstood.

The dog of legend is the epitome of courage and fidelity. The hound of Montdidier seeks out the murderer Macaire with unfailing certainty and fights a death duel with its master's assassin. Greyfriars Bobby carries his fidelity to even greater lengths and pines away upon the grave of its master. Balto, the sled-dog hero of the 'diphtheria run,' apparently displays a perspicacity to put its owner to shame and a knowledge of tidal movements that would have delighted Henry the Navigator.

Dog heroes of literature are even more sensible and perspicacious. Robert Michael Ballantyne's *The Dog Crusoe* (incidentally this epic tale of a Landseer Newfoundland is reputed to be one of the books that has inspired more dog-trainers than any work of fiction ever written) tells of a dog that has the innate bush craft of a Fenimore Cooper hero, the wisdom of Solomon and the ability to see a connection between the general and the particular concept that would be the envy of a Schopenhauer.

Dawson's *Finn, an Irish Wolfhound* is a truly wonderful hound which not only adapts to a feral Australasian life better than the native-bred dingoes, but even after a year of living in the wild remembers his one-time master and fights off the pack mates which are hell bent on destroying the man. Finn is not only more intelligent than the kangaroo hound he replaces, but considerably brighter than the Antipodean dingo hunter who adopts him, and literally streets ahead of his original Pommy owner who stumbles around in the bush without map or compass.

Jack London's canine superheroes are even more remarkable – possibly because London knew little of dogs and owned but two during his entire lifetime. Buck, the hero of *The Call of the Wild*, a mongrel St Bernard/sheepdog mix (London spent a winter in the Yukon holed up with Marshall and Louis Bond who owned such a cross-breed) adapts remarkably to Arctic conditions despite being reared in California, becomes a better sled dog than a native-bred husky, sorts out good from bad in the manner of a Colin Wilson psychiatrist and finally reverts to the wild, mates with timber wolves and is careful to wreak havoc only on the tribes of Indians who killed his master.

Jack London's penultimate book, *Jerry of the Islands*, displays the author's xenophobia and contempt for any race that cannot be categorised as White Anglo-Saxon Protestant and once again the hero Jerry, an Irish terrier, is loyal, intelligent and wonderfully clever at detecting native-bred villains even after its master has come to trust the Kanakas. London was unbelievably anthropomorphic and credited his canine heroes with human qualities or rather superhuman qualities for the dogs of London's novels were invariably a cut above the low grade humans who owned them. Yet despite this, London did in fact bring about great improvements in the training of performing dogs and other circus animals. In the sequel to *Jerry of the Islands – Michael, Brother of Jerry* – London describes the inhuman treatment of circus animals and performing dog troupes so vividly that Jack London Clubs were set up to picket animal acts that were known to use cruelty to train the performers.

Attributing a certain nobility to dogs, particularly wild canids, was a popular pathetic fallacy used in many American novels. Zane Grey, who knew London (and Sinclair Lewis who had furnished the plots of many of London's books), also attributes the dog and its wild relatives with a curious nobility. In his short story 'The Wolf Tracker', Brink, an embittered bounty hunter, runs down a killer wolf and strangles it only to return to civilisation to reject his bounty and to remark on the courage and nobility of the wild canid and the cowardice of man. It has been said by Damon Runyon that Zane Grey's contempt for man's cowardice was due to the fact that Zane Grey had once trained as a dentist!

Although such tales are exciting, and certainly well worth reading, they give a most inaccurate account of the nature of the dog. Dogs simply do not think like human beings nor is their behaviour governed by man's notions of fair play, honour and decency (though the inbuilt codes that govern canine conduct are even more rigid than those that govern or shape human behaviour). In fact if the would-be dog-buyer expects his purchase to behave or think in the manner of the dog heroes of literature he would be wise to forget buying a particular breed of dog or obtaining and training any breed of dog, for that matter.

Dogs can be trained to a very high standard, but no dog possesses human intelligence, and to expect any dog to have the commonsense, honour and decency manifested by the dogs portrayed in legend or fiction is to court disaster. Sadly, tales of canine superheroes of particular breeds often influence a would-be dog-owner to purchase a puppy of the same breed and expect it to behave in the manner of the fictional superdog. This line of thinking inevitably leads to a very disappointed owner and, what is worse, a very disenchanted and dispirited dog! Read the books, enjoy the author's style and the tale he has to tell, but such tales alone should not influence a buyer to purchase a puppy – nor should such novels act as a guide to the training of the whelp one has purchased. The superdogs of fiction belong in the pages of books and are seldom encountered in reality.

4

Dogs or Bitches?

One of my favourite characters was a dog-dealer called Jim Spuckley who despite the fact that his kennels were deplorable and his ideas on dogs baffling and inaccurate, kept his wards in superb condition. Spuckley wove epigrams like a skilled weaver weaves cloth, and he had glib sayings to suit all situations. Over the period of the two or three months I knew him I watched him advise clients that dogs were easier to train than bitches and next week that bitches were infinitely more biddable than dogs. Baffled by Spuckley's fickle advice, I questioned him about it. He thought a moment, twitched his face furiously and replied, 'If I've got dogs for sale, I tell 'em buy a dog. If I've got bitches, I say buy a bitch. If I've got nowt for sale I says don't buy a dog or bitches – they're a bloody nuisance', and if this is not an enigmatic introduction to a chapter, I don't know what is.

Yet first-time dog-buyers must often ask breeders for advice about whether to buy a dog or a bitch and the replies they receive are often motivated by availability. To advise a potential buyer on whether dog or bitch is easier to train is difficulty, if not impossible. I succeed in training bitches more easily than I train dogs, while my co-trainer has a greater affinity with male canines.

As a general rule, bitches are less dominant than dogs from

the same litter, though while still in the nest a whole litter may well submit to a bitch puppy. In 1989 I reared a litter of German shepherd dog puppies from an extremely docile bitch mated to her own son – an incestuously bred litter that I hoped would breed out the hip dysplasia problem that was troubling my kennel at that time. As the litter grew I developed diabetes and my time spent with the whelps shortened until it consisted of a three-meal-a-day visit to the kennels which were cleaned out by a rather unobservant kennel lad. As soon as I felt slightly better I began spending more time in the kennels and I noticed that one large fat whelp stood out in a litter of rather puny litter-mates. My kennel lad explained – 'only about half the food is ever eaten'. I sat and watched the litter feed and realised both why the one bitch puppy was larger than her mates and the reason for the half-eaten plates of meal and meat. At feeding time the bitch guarded the plates fiercely, rushing from dish to dish and attacking the whelps, preventing them from feeding. Shepherd puppies are so easily subdued by an aggressive litter-mate that they had tolerated this extremely dominant bitch and her bossy ways. I took her away from the litter at feeding times and in days the litter started to gain weight but I had some doubt about placing the six-week-old fiend that dominated her siblings and had I not been ill at the time I would have been morally obliged to keep her and attempt to train her, for I am reluctant to place an extremely dominant animal of any sort with a family, lest the dog literally begins to rule the household. The reader would be surprised to find out just how many families live in slight fear of the dog they own!

Luck (seldom a visitor to my house I'm afraid) was with me in placing the puppy and she went to an obedience and agility trainer who assured the bitch of her epsilon rank in the household and she became an adoring family pet who submits to the rough handling of the smallest child in the trainer's family.

Bitches are seldom as dominant as are dogs of the same litter and more easily slot into the human pack at their position of the lowest and most submissive member. During the years when I took on difficult dogs for retraining, I was seldom brought bitches that had sought to rule the roost in the home they shared with a human family, but the number of male dogs that had assumed a dominant role in the mixed human/canine household were legion. I had some small success with these dogs, but I confess I failed dismally with many. Perhaps, were I not such an epsilon level person myself, my success rate with these dogs would have been much higher.

Canids are naturally gregarious animals and thus obey strict social codes to establish an equilibrium within the pack. Many cynologists believe that bitches occupy the most important role in the pack situation and that they determine the way a hunt will take place. My own opinion is that theories of this nature have been conceived and proven under unnatural laboratory conditions and do not represent the way packs behave. My theories are based on observations made when I hunted a terrier pack of some thirty to sixty terriers. As soon as two or more dogs congregate together and form what must be loosely described as a pack, that pack stratifies into hunters that seek out and drive the game and catch dogs that are strong enough to bring the quarry down. As most packs are simply extended families descended from one bitch, her role of hunter-seeker has long been accepted by her children and grandchildren and her position as pack organiser, so to speak, has virtually nothing to do with her position in the law of peck that governs the pack's day-to-day social behaviour. However, if I might act as a Devil's advocate, I must admit that my terrier pack was composed of bitches that showed a greater propensity to hunt up quarry and the males were usually the more eager catch dogs. Why certain people succeed best at training male dogs while others perform better with bitches has been the subject of much debate. It is likely that because I am a fairly submissive sort of character I unintentionally select animals that are also slightly submissive and this theory was suggested by Dr Robert Hanks, a student of the relationship between men and the animals he has sought to domesticate. My lurchers, a strain I have bred since childhood, are very submissive and sycophantic, more so than any other strain of lurcher in fact, so Hanks may well be fairly accurate in his hypothesis.

A slightly more avant garde theory has been put forward by various sporting periodicals during the 1980s. Dogs and humans both emit scents that are seemingly undetectable except by complex scientific instruments, but have a great importance in the day-to-day life of either species. These esters, referred to as pheromones, may well determine why certain people succeed at job interviews while others do not – they may also play an important part in why certain women and men are sexually attracted to one another – and this pheromone attraction theory has been substantiated by a series of laboratory tests that were financed by perfume manufacturers.

It was, one supposes, an almost inevitable progression that behaviourists concerned with the interaction between man and animals should begin to explore the importance of pheromones in this relationship. In fact, there is some evidence that manufacturers of livestock husbandry products may have pre-empted cosmetic manufacturers in their researches into the importance of scent in sexual attraction as the various synthetic boar scents used by pig breeders attest. At the time of writing there are some field sports writers who state that they believe that the pheromones emitted by both human beings and dogs may determine why some people find it easier to train bitches than dogs and vice versa. I certainly don't feel qualified to enter into such a debate. Enough however of wild surmise. Kipling, who did more than imply that the female of the species was deadlier than the male, was perhaps correct in his assumption, yet few guard dog trainers will consider training bitches for security work. Nonetheless bitches are often fearsome guards. When I lived in Huddlesford near Lichfield my house was situated on a bend of the road and could not be seen by any of my neighbours. It was not only an idyllic setting but an ideal spot to burgle! My house was ransacked with such regularity that at one time I contemplated leaving my front door unlocked. I became thoroughly disenchanted with our local police force (though at one time they did set up alarm systems in my house) and eventually I resorted to covering my windows with steel mesh and using a variety of other anti-burglar devices. These deterrents were to no avail and my bitterness towards our local police increased. National newspapers with reporters who were even more antipathetic to the police wrote copiously on my plight and for a short while afterwards my burglaries abated. Yet during the winter of 1979 they resumed their former intensity and frequency. Soon there was little left to steal but still, most weeks I would arrive home from work to find the lock of my front door kicked in and my place ransacked and at the risk of being accused of indelicacy a disgusting 'calling card' that is the hallmark of the maladjusted criminal, left behind.

I hired a large male dobermann – one of the biggest I could find, and for a while tolerated the stench of urine that greeted me when I returned from school for the dog sprayed furniture and corners alike. Though he literally wrecked my house and chewed furniture and my clothes with regularity, he did deter burglars. One day I returned home to find my dobermann greeting me cordially as I left my car, but my front door almost kicked to pieces by thieves who had now clearly called my bluff and tested the prowess of the dobermann. To say this stage marked the lowest point of my life would not be an understatement for I have never experienced despair such as I felt on that occasion.

I wrote a furious letter to the Chief Constable, an equally bitter one to a national newspaper and returned the dobermann to its owner. On the advice of a one-time police dog handler friend I bought a white German shepherd dog bitch and because of the spate of publicity and the fact that my house was supposedly wired like Fort Knox I had a fairly burglar-free year, though my terriers were stolen so regularly that it was futile to contemplate breeding a litter.

In the meanwhile, Polly, my German shepherd dog bitch, grew to maturity. Her gentle, rather serious disposition did not impress me at first and I mistook her reserved attitude with strangers for nervousness. She trained so easily that it was almost as if someone had previously taught her basic obedience and such was her curious maternal instinct that when one of my terriers attacked a young piglet and nearly killed it, Polly, observing the distress of the piglet that lay in a box next to the fire in my living room (one could scarcely imagine a less desirable room mate, though the piglet was considerably cleaner than the dobermann) the bitch came into milk and suckled the piglet.

Her gentle, amicable disposition was however deceptive. One Sunday she allowed two of my six-and seven-year-old god-daughters to dress her in skirts and blouses. The Monday following the abuse of the ever tolerant Polly I arrived home to find my door kicked in yet again and a fearfully injured, blood-bespattered Polly lying against the warm sides of my Rayburn. The house was as daubed with blood as the hut of Llewellyn who slew the luckless hound Gelert. I lifted Polly gently, placed her in the car and rushed her to my vet in Lichfield, but while it transpired that Polly had broken several ribs, she had no wounds that could have seeped such a quantity of gore. My feelings could best be described as a combination of satisfaction and terror of being prosecuted for owning a dangerous dog and in panic I phoned Eddie Judd who had first advised the purchase of Polly. His advice was sensible and cryptic – 'First, a little blood goes a long way' (a common expression in the world of professional boxing) 'and second, if Polly has done severe damage you will know about it soon enough, believe me!' On that note Eddie rang off leaving me to live out a rather anxious week when I expected a call from the police at any moment. For once my tale has a happy ending – the burglaries ceased as suddenly as they had started – and I have never regretted the purchase of that recently deceased bitch.

Guard dog trainers and handlers are usually less willing to train a bitch than a dog simply because dogs are larger, stronger and hence have a greater deterrent value to would-be attackers or trespassers than bitches.

Bitches, at least healthy bitches or bitches which are not

jealous guards of young puppies, are usually less prone to biting people than are dogs of the same breed – and I must qualify such a statement forthwith before proceeding further. During the days when I strove to create the Plummer terrier – a totally new breed of working terrier – I produced many surplus puppies that were physically sound, but not what I required to continue the bloodline. Hence I gave away dozens of puppies – dogs and bitches alike – to anyone who would offer the puppy a good home. Terriers are often aggressive dogs that need work to keep them mentally and physically sound and hence the terriers I gave to pet homes often began to behave badly or became rather unpleasant stock-worriers and, worse still, child-biters. Over a period of twenty years I was called to rehouse thirty-five terriers most of which I put to hunt service with local fox hound packs. Yet only one bitch, a terrier puppy I called Coin, was returned when her owners considered her to be 'snappy'. As it transpired, she returned to me when she was twelve weeks of age and when I touched her food dish she menaced me and then sank her milk teeth into my hand. I lifted her clear off the ground, shook her and then put her back to the food dish. Once more I attempted to remove the dish and once more she drew tiny pinpricks of blood on my hands. I lifted her, shook her violently and replaced her near the dish. She never again retaliated or warned me or growled at me and when she was put to hunt service she became very much part of the hunt terrier man's family and devoted to the terrier man's daughter. Yet some of the dogs that were 'returned' remained unruly devils with children.

I make no apology for the fact that this chapter has offered no hard and fast advice as to whether dogs are preferable to bitches when it comes to training. I prefer training bitches. My co-trainer finds dogs more easy to control. Yer pays yer money and takes yer choice – or so it seems.

5

Should One Buy A Puppy or An Adult Dog?

In a matter of minutes I must set out to sea to haul in my nets and check my crab creels – though 1991 has been such a poor year, catchwise, that my forthcoming labours are hardly likely to be worth the effort involved. To get to the harbour I must start my rather dilapidated diesel van that has not only seen better days but also seen a great variety of owners, ranging from the somewhat less meticulous owner to owners who neglected to change the oil, to those who failed to observe damage to the cooling system, and possibly those who must have used some peculiar mixture of cheap poor-grade fuels. The van has suffered accordingly. It starts quite easily some days. On other days it is a shade more reluctant to fire. Sometimes it steadfastly refuses to start or runs sulkily as if resentful of the awful treatment it has received over the last five or six years. Automobiles seldom improve if they are passed from hand to hand to be abused by a great variety of owners and in this respect dogs are very much like motor vehicles.

Now while I confess I have had a great variety of secondhand cars – some bad and some even worse – I am reluctant to undertake and train a secondhand dog if I am able to obtain a puppy of the same breed at a reasonable price. A puppy straight from the nest bought at some eight weeks of age is usually so malleable and ductile that it can be shaped, made or marred by the owner/trainer. An older dog – particularly if the said dog has, like William James' thirty-year-old man, 'had its character set like cement' – will be less easy to shape or train.

At the time of writing, most breed clubs sponsor breed rescue societies which rehouse adult dogs and while I am the first to admit that these breed rescue societies perform a wonderful service and often provide animals with suitable homes and suitable owners, I would certainly not recommend that a person who is not *au fait* with the training of a dog takes on one of these rescue society animals in preference to an unspoilt puppy of the same breed, though once again I have to say I have great respect for any person who obtains one of these rescue society adult dogs, trains and makes a success of the animal. However, having said that I would not consider taking on a breed rescue society adult dog (that is almost certainly likely to be 'almost' free to a good home as well as inoculated against the four major canine ills) it behoves me to say exactly why I would be chary about taking on such an adult dog.

First, I would be interested in knowing why a dog has come to rest at one of these breed rescue society kennels and even more interested in the events that preceded the dog's arrival at such an establishment. It is possible, just possible, that the owner of the said dog has died and the animal just has to be rehoused. It is also just possible that the owner of the dog now residing in these rescue society kennels has had to go abroad or to spend a lengthy spell in hospital and hence is unable to take the dog with him or her. It is also possible that the dog waiting to be rehoused is sane, sensible, unmarred by stupid or brutal treatment and likely to be an absolute treasure to own.

Conversely, and this is more than just possible, I am afraid, the dog has, since it left its breeder, experienced one heck of a raw deal from life and new owner alike. Like as not the animal has been purchased by a totally unsuitable owner, who has taken a stab at training the dog, failed miserably and given the dog away, vowing never again to own such a dog again or possibly never to own another dog of any kind. Some of the dogs waiting to be rehoused will be home-wreckers and, lest the reader misconstrues what I've said, I shall explain this statement more fully. Many dogs are treated in such a way that they become very insecure and cannot be left in the house without attacking the furniture, walls and flooring with the gusto of a demolition squad. Such dogs can and will destroy a home and turn a perfectly acceptable house into a hovel minutes after the owner has left the residence.

Car-chasers, cat-killers, neurotics and biters are often to be found at these kennels but the majority of the resident adult dogs are dispirited, confused animals that were once basically sound, healthy and happy puppies purchased by people who knew little about dog behaviour and dog training or, worse still, have heeded the advice of people who know even less about the said subjects. I groan aloud when the owner of a badly trained, bewildered lurcher tells me he has been taught all he needs to know about dogs by an 'old poacher', for many old poachers tell a newcomer such tales of hocus pocus that it is virtually impossible to train a dog using the methods suggested. Worse still, it is virtually impossible to retrain an owner that has heeded such claptrap.

It is also a fact that while some breeds such as greyhounds, German shepherd dogs, spaniels and retrievers, take to new owners fairly easily and suffer little mental damage in the process, other breeds are more damaged by the change of ownership and may develop additional peculiarities and hang-ups because of this change of ownership. Lorenz and Terasse both mention that chow chows (and possibly other Spitz breeds) dislike changes of ownership and often resent or ignore their new owners. Lorenz uses this fact to explain why he believes that chow chows are lupine types or a breed derived from wolf stock and wolves are rarely accepted into the social structures of new packs, nor do they seem to wish to mingle with strange wolves. German shepherd dogs, however (or so Lorenz believes) are jackal-blooded dogs descended from the golden jackal, and jackals enjoy a rather more loose pack structure than do wolves. It would be almost sacrilege to contradict a Nobel Prize winner of the calibre of Lorenz, but while it may be true that chow chows are reluctant to accept new owners, the same cannot be said for Spitz-blooded sled dogs. Whole teams can be sold by an owner and work for the buyer quite as readily as they did for their original owner/trainer. However, it may well be that a sled dog team represents a mini pack (and the subsequent social structure that exists within that mini pack is already well defined) and this buffers the shock of the change of ownership. Individual sled dogs brought into existing teams however take only a matter of hours to accept new ownership and new team companions.

It seems a strange irony, but at the time of writing, the most commonly 'swapped', changed and passed-on pure breed of dog is certainly the saluki, as a glance at the advertisement column of sporting newspapers attests. These curious, remote Middle-Eastern hounds (and their hybrids known as lurchers or longdogs) are in fact the stock in trade of down-market dog dealers. Yet no breed of dog craves human affection or demands human contact as much as does the saluki or one of the allied breeds of Middle-Eastern hounds. Such hounds, once used to human contact, suffer badly in kennels while waiting to be rehoused, despite the fact that their rather blank, stoical stares may give little indication of the mental hell they may experience as they are passed from home to home by uncaring dog-dealers. Paul Sagar, a successful coursing saluki enthusiast, is of the opinion that a saluki takes a few years to blend into a relationship with its owner/trainer and hence the constant chopping and changing that many dealers require a saluki to endure has a disastrous effect on its mental make-up. Sagar is also of the opinion that the curious reaction of many salukis and saluki hybrids fielded by match runners, many of whom have only an ephemeral interest in the hounds and simply pass them on to new homes if the hound doesn't perform well, may well be due to the saluki's need for permanent and loving ownership. Salukis and saluki longdogs have the reputation for being some of the most capricious dogs and seem to behave erratically and perhaps irrationally at certain times. Jacqui Saunders of Poulton Engine, Bristol, one of the European authorities on the allied type, the sloughi or Berber greyhound, shares Sagar's notions concerning the need of these hounds for stability. Bitter experience has taught Miss Saunders that perhaps it is better to have a sloughi put down rather than allow it to pass from home to home and become more and more mentally scarred by the many changes of ownership. The Middle-Eastern sight hound's need for stability may well be offered as the reason why Arabs are reluctant to sell adult salukis – though it is equally likely that the tales of Arabs refusing to sell their hounds are due to the fact that few dog-lovers of any race are willing to sell dogs to which they have become emotionally attached.

It has to be mentioned that at one time there was a considerable market for grown dogs, or to be more precise 'dogs over distemper', for prior to 1948 and the Laidlaw and Dunkin research into the subject of distemper and the classification of the viruses that caused the malaise, distemper was the scourge of young dogs of all breeds. Dog periodicals bristled with adverts for panaceas and prophylactic measures that supposedly would ward off the dreaded virus that caused the illness. Lucas (1931) advertised a concoction called Lucanis that he claimed would enable a dog to recover from the most virulent forms of the disease, but until the perfection of the vaccine, distemper was the scourge of dogdom. Puppies were more susceptible to the disease than were adults and hence dogs which were mature and 'over distemper' often fetched a higher price than did puppies of the same breed. These days distemper is now less common though it has by no means been eradicated in the same way as smallpox (though I believe it could be) and inoculations against this dreadful infection have not only made the purchase of puppies a somewhat safer business than it once was, but also has made the sale of grown dogs a less profitable business.

Young or sapling dogs (dogs under eighteen months of age) are usually readily available from breeders who specialise in producing exhibition stock. These animals were once puppies which had either shown terrific show potential and not lived up to their early promise as exhibition-type animals or they are whelps that were run on simply because the breeder had failed to sell them as puppies. If these saplings have been house-reared properly, socialised and received some basic preliminary training they may well adapt to the lifestyle of the typical pet dog owner. If the puppy has lived out its infancy in kennels, become remote or has not been socialised, the prospect of such a whelp settling into the typical pet home is less promising though some clients are obviously quite happy about the purchase of sub-exhibition-standard sapling dogs.

Personally, if offered a house-trained, fully inoculated sapling for the same price as a puppy, I would buy the puppy every time for it is considerably easier to train an unspoilt puppy than to eradicate training faults and peculiar or irritating mannerisms that have manifested themselves in a sapling that has been reared, socialised and trained by someone else.

6

Rudimentary Puppy-Training

So let us assume that the reader has visited a dog-breeder and secured a puppy of his or her choice and taken it home. Let me also assume the reader is a first-time dog-owner and has little or no experience of settling in a puppy. If this is so, the reader must expect the puppy's first night in its new home to be one of the most unpleasant imaginable. It is a sad fact that many buyers who purchase a whelp will either phone for advice the morning after the purchase or, in extreme cases, return the puppy to the breeder and either ask for their money to be refunded or, if that first night with the puppy has been particularly traumatic, offer to return the whelp free of charge and be so keen to hightail it off the breeder's premises that they would willingly have paid the breeder to take back the puppy.

I assure the reader what I have stated is the absolute truth. During the time when I endeavoured to produce a true breeding strain of terrier, I bred many surplus puppies and these I advertised at quite a low price in order to place them in happy permanent homes. Dog breeding is certainly not all beer and skittles and one of the most irritating aspects of the trade is the after-sales service demanded by many buyers. Despite the advice I insisted a potential buyer should endure, three out of every five buyers phoned me early next morning to state that they had endured a night that was little short of purgatory because of the antics of the newly purchased puppy. One out of every fifteen clients – and the reader must now realise I keep a very accurate diary – returned the puppy and, because of the low price I asked for my whelps, many even declined the offer to refund their purchase price, so grateful were they to be rid of the whelps. One client, finding I was not at home, even forced open my porch door and left the puppy in a box in the said porch – and 'like the fabric of the vision faded, vanished' and I never saw or heard from the man again. It now seems I must explain why many of my clients reacted so strangely to their first night with a new puppy – and, reader, in no way have I exaggerated the bedlam I began to expect the morning after I sold a puppy to an apparently normal and healthy family.

Puppies are naturally sociable animals, they enjoy being in the company of other dogs or human beings. Breeders usually endeavour to take the bitch away from the litter (seldom the litter away from the bitch) when the puppies are six or seven weeks of age in order that the puppies can be sold at eight weeks. After that time the puppy's immunity begins to wane and this necessitates a fairly expensive series of inoculations against the major ills that can plague young puppies.

At this age the puppy will derive great pleasure from playing with its litter-mates and from the warmth emitted by the dams of these puppies. Puppies do in fact invariably choose to sleep sprawled on top of one another rather than find an unoccupied space to spend their sleeping hours.

A puppy so reared now reaches the age of eight weeks and is sold to a buyer who intends to keep and rear the puppy in the buyer's house. The sheer novelty of owning a puppy will invariably encourage the buyer to play with his new acquisition and, for the evening at least, the puppy – who incidentally will enjoy the attention – will appear to settle into the routine of family life. At this stage it is not uncommon for the buyer to be so delighted with his purchase that he will phone the breeder to say how happy he is with his puppy. If the vendor has an iota of decency, he or she will warn the buyer that the night ahead may well be traumatic for both the puppy and the family, and will remind the buyer of the recommended remedies for reducing this trauma.

The family now prepares to retire for the night, and quite suddenly the puppy finds itself in darkness and experiences the same loneliness and despair as did the victim in H. G. Wells' *The New Catacomb*. Never has the puppy been as lonely, and never has it experienced such fear and confusion. For a minute or so the puppy may silently snuffle around the darkened room, seeking the scents of his litter-mates and the warmth and security offered by its fellow puppies, but, when it fails to find a trace of its litter-mates, or of its human owners that have vanished without trace and plunged the room into total darkness, it will express its anxiety and fears vocally by either barking frantically or howling loudly – an action which not only expresses the puppy's unhappiness but is designed to attract members of the mini-dog-pack – the dam and her litter – to the plight of a lost puppy.

It has been scientifically proven that the cry of a human baby is so pitched that the mother of the child finds it impossible to ignore or blot out the cry of the unhappy infant and tests have shown that even women in deep sleep react to the cries of their own children. At the risk of being totally unscientific, I would suggest that several thousand years of domestication of the dog has produced a curious reciprocity between man and dog, for whereas many dogs react excitedly and unhappily to the cries or moans of a human in distress (this reaction is certainly utilised by trainers of dogs used to seek out survivors trapped in the rubble after bombing raids), human beings too find it desperately difficult to ignore the cries of a puppy in distress.

So upset will some owners become that they will leave their beds to go and comfort the unhappy whelp; after making a fuss of it and calming its fears they promptly vanish again, thereby exacerbating the puppy's confusion and loneliness. Worse still, the owner might become so upset by the puppy's cries that he or she may decide to take the puppy to the bedroom so that it can spend the night with its new owners. This is a disastrous mistake for it now becomes doubly difficult to accustom the puppy to being left alone in the future. On no account should the new owner relent and take the whelp to his or her bedroom, though I admit that the plaintive bleat of a puppy has such a disturbing effect that it is very difficult to resist.

Make no bones about it, the first night a puppy spends with its new owner can be upsetting to say the least and responsible breeders should warn potential purchasers of the possible problems. While there is no certain method of ensuring that owners of a newly purchased puppy will not be disturbed or upset by its plaintive bleating, various methods may make the puppy feel a little more secure and therefore a little less vocal.

Some breeders suggest that a puppy should be given a box or basket with a hot water bottle in it. The reasoning behind this notion is that the puppy experiences some sense of security from the warmth emitted by its litter-mates and the hot water bottle acts as a surrogate litter-mate. Many new owners report great success using this method. Others suggest that the purchase of a loud ticking clock (the sort of noisy cheap alarm clock obtainable from most hardware stores) is more efficient.

While it is relatively easy to explain why a hot water bottle may have a calming effect on a newly purchased puppy, it is a little more difficult to explain why the presence of a clock in the room should be efficacious in any way. It has been argued that the sound of a clock ticking resembles the sound of the beating heart of the puppy's dam. This is clearly ridiculous as there is little or no resemblance between the sound of a clock and the beating of a mammalian heart – despite the theory having prompted novels by both Poe and Lovecraft. Yet many dog-owners report on the therapeutic effect the sound of a clock has on the puppy. In all probability the ticking, accentuated by the silence of the darkened house, excites some interest in the whelp and helps ease the monotony and loneliness of the first night away from its litter mates.

I am naturally sceptical about rustic wisdom – old poachers' training methods, or the wisdom of travelling folk – but one of the most astute dog-trainers I have ever met was a settled Romany called Moses Aaron Smith. Moses was not only a great raconteur – Radio Derby made good use of his tales at one time – but he possessed a homespun wisdom that is seldom encountered these days. He boasted that he had never experienced a moment's trouble with a newly acquired puppy simply because he always lined the puppy's basket with an unwashed old coat, jacket or shirt. I confess that I find this method of settling a puppy has little to commend it but I can understand Moses' logic. When a young dog is left alone in a room for the first time it often wreaks havoc, micturating and defecating all too freely and often damaging the furniture, flooring and walls of the room. However at some stage prior to the young dog's attack on furnishings and walls it will usually try to drag out some article of human apparel and attempt to lie on it, as if the presence of a strong scent of human being (and apparently we are a lot more aromatic than we care to admit – Corbett believes that our odious stench usually deters large predators such as lions and tigers) has a soothing effect on the puppy.

It is also interesting that coursers who use salukis or hybrid forms of salukis known as longdogs often have great difficulty recovering their wards after a course, for instead of returning to hand after a fruitless course (as would a well-trained lurcher), salukis and saluki composites are wont to seek out other quarry and hunt on yet further away from their handler. Many saluki owners are sensible enough not to chase after their hounds – and it would require a very athletic person to catch a saluki anyway – but simply leave an old jacket or heavily scented garment near to the point where the saluki first 'sprung' its hare. It is not uncommon for the saluki-owner to return to find the wayward hound sitting on the garment waiting for the owner. The familiar scent has offered some security to a hound that is now very lost and very confused.

If the owner of the newly acquired puppy already has another dog – provided it shows no antipathy to the new arrival – then the presence of another dog usually ensures that the whelp feels secure, and the owner of the puppy will not experience a distressing, sleepless night. A word of warning is necessary at this point. Few older dogs are antipathetic to a new puppy, but should the older dog display any animosity to the whelp it is extremely unwise to leave them alone together. Hostility to the puppy may be demonstrated in various ways. The older dog may growl or show its teeth when the puppy approaches it, but a more perplexing sign that all will not be well during the forthcoming night is when the older dog moves from place to place to escape the attentions of the pestering puppy. The chances are that when the adult dog has no place where it can escape from the attentions of the puppy it will retaliate, sometimes with great ferocity.

Hancock of Sutton Coldfield, the world's most successful lurcher breeder, tells an interesting tale to illustrate this point. He had sold an eight-week-old lurcher puppy to a man who owned a cross-bred bull terrier x fell terrier – a formidable mix by any standards – and the purchaser had allowed the two dogs to stay in the small kitchen of his council house. The lurcher puppy had pestered the terrier until the owner came downstairs to find the terrier standing on the draining board menacing the puppy that was trying to befriend it. The owner of the pair had not heeded the all-too-obvious warning signs; and in the morning he found the terrier perched on a window ledge and the lurcher puppy quite dead lying on the kitchen floor.

A puppy is seldom unwilling to be left alone once it has settled into its new home, though it may become extremely destructive with furnishings and in particular with any shoes its owner has left in the same room. It is always a good policy to check the room in which a puppy is to be left for any length of time. Curtains should be lifted out of the puppy's reach, and valuable furniture, ornaments and shoes removed from the room. Certain pet food manufacturers produce chewy hide strips to occupy the puppy's attention while the owner is absent, many of which are produced in the shape of a child's shoe. These pieces of hide certainly reduce the damage a puppy will cause if left alone, but an old shoe usually occupies its attention just as well and allows it to give vent to its destructive desires. It is highly unlikely that a dog's sense of aesthetics will be similar to our own, as the variety of misshapen objects my terriers regularly carry to my door attests. Whereas a householder might consider that a torn and chewed shoe in the dog basket looks unsightly, the puppy might consider the object to be a treasured toy. It is unnecessary to buy expensive toys for dogs: not only do puppies in particular find highly scented, discarded shoes far more appealing than colourful supermarket dog toys – but they alter the shape of their dog toys within minutes of their being given to them. Teething puppies are said to be more destructive than younger or older whelps, but the damage even a newly weaned puppy may cause is often quite distressing to the house-proud owner.

It seems only yesterday that we were subjected to the absurd cult that decreed that neither animals nor children should be restricted in any way lest this damaged their psychological development. It was during the late 1960s that this quasi-scientific theory was believed by many. Children were allowed to express their every emotion regardless of the hurt they perpetrated on adults, growing into such loathsome brats that an older generation once again came to think that only conscription would curb teenagers reared without any form of restraint. It is even more surprising that some dog-breeders emulated these ludicrous no-restraint notions, advocating that dogs should not be house-trained by conventional methods but should be allowed to explore their environment and 'discover' that the house was not the best place to soil or foul. Thankfully the notion was a short-lived one, and I met only one person who believed that the deliberate house-training of a dog damaged certain aspects of its mental development. The tale is too good not to be included here.

During the late 1960s I had many dogs, but refrained from keeping any indoors. I had lived a bachelor-type existence for several years and while penury ensured I was never exactly house-proud, I was only too aware of how quickly a dog kept indoors could change a house into a hovel. My association with a woman who had an interest in toy breeds did however bring me into contact with the most amazing eccentric I have ever met.

We went to stay with a breeder of toy dogs, who lived in a large, swish, upper-middle-class estate in a town in the south of England. Outwardly the detached house looked no different from those adjacent to it, but when our hostess opened the door the most appalling stench I have ever encountered struck me in the face, causing my eyes to water. Lest the reader should believe I am an effete sort of person and that I have exaggerated the potency of this nauseating stench, I must add that at that time I was hunting a terrier pack to rat in poultry farms, knacker's yards and even a maggot factory. Yet never has such a stench assailed my nostrils as when the hostess opened her front door.

She kept some twenty-three tiny dogs ranging from papillons to miniature poodles. While I found these some of the most charming little dogs I have ever encountered, not one had been house-trained and the living room was daubed and stained with excrement. The notion that dogs should either house-train themselves or not house-train at all, had obviously been recently acquired: the expensive furniture, while it stank of dog excrement, wasn't particularly damaged, though a succession of stud dogs lifting their legs against the base of a polished teak table had caused the French polish to blister. It was the most awful place, yet our hostess seemed totally oblivious.

I'm afraid most dog-keepers ignore the stench caused by badly house-trained dogs, and it must come as an unpleasant surprise when someone has the temerity to remark on it. Yet while it is impossible to completely rid the house of the smell of a dog living there; it is a relatively easy process to house-train a puppy of any breed.

Many methods of house-and toilet-training dogs and young children literally smack of witchcraft. During the Middle Ages apothecaries often advocated that a bedwetting child could be cured by being made to swallow a live mouse – and if the belief astonishes and horrifies the reader, it should be pointed out that such a notion is no more ludicrous than the theory that a puppy should be house-trained by rubbing its nose in the excrement it has just passed. Yet such an absurd notion survives to the present day and may have lent some substance to the 'no house-train notion' of the late 1960s: the action of rubbing a puppy's nose in its own filth must be mentally perplexing to both the puppy and any thinking person watching the exercise.

For the life of me I have never understood why any normal person could believe that a puppy can make the connection between the action of having its face rubbed in filth and developing the habit of fouling out of doors and not in the house. Perhaps the dog-owner who perpetrates this absurd and pointless piece of cruelty believes that if the dog is shown that its body wastes are objectionable to the owner it will seek to pass them in a place where its owner is unable to find them. I make no apology for what must seem a lavatorial discourse, for I believe many young puppies are mentally scarred by this all-too-common practice. Whenever I sold surplus terrier puppies I always asked potential clients how they intended to house-train the puppy. If they answered that they rubbed the dog's nose in its filth I refused to sell them a puppy. The hyperactive nature of a typical terrier makes the breed a less than satisfactory house pet anyway, even without an owner who mentally scars the puppy by daubing its nose in its own filth.

How, therefore, should a puppy be house-trained? Frankly, house-training a normal, healthy whelp is, or should be, simplicity itself, if, that is, the owner is constantly with the puppy and does not spend most of the day away from the house – when such conditions occur it is often very difficult to house-train a puppy.

Puppies are very much creatures of habit. Seconds after they wake up – and young puppies sleep a great deal of the time – they seek to urinate. A minute or so after feeding they also pass urine, and often seek to defecate. Thus as soon as a puppy wakes it should be taken up gently and placed out of doors on a suitable spot. Immediately the puppy has fed the same process should be repeated, and the puppy not allowed to foul or urinate in any other place other than the one designated by its owner.

Most mammals can be house-trained by these methods. In 1983 I trained a Duroc piglet to sit, stay, and fetch a ball like Slut, the famous eighteen-century pointing and retrieving pig. She performed these tasks as readily as a dog. While a piglet she regularly came into the house, and was trained to foul and urinate on a patch of dry leaves near the house. She house-trained as easily as would an intelligent puppy, but the tale has a rather unpleasant ending. Although she approached 200 pounds in weight and was even stronger than one would expect from such an animal, she was still allowed to come into the house. One day a phone call delayed my letting her out to foul, and she smashed and tore an expensive ornamental door in order to get to her patch of leaves.

Many trainers advocate paper-training, and many flat-dwellers own dogs that have been so conditioned to foul only on newspaper that when out walking with their owners they show great anxiety to return to their pads of paper to foul or urinate. Paper-training is quite simply a variation of the house-training described above. When the puppy wakes up or finishes eating or drinking, it is placed on a pad of newspaper and gently restrained until it urinates or defecates. This operation is repeated every time the whelp wakes or feeds, until it accepts the pad as the only place to evacuate its bowels and its bladder.

Many pet-owners use the paper pad process to encourage the puppy to foul and urinate outside the house. The pad of paper is placed in a spot the puppy is known to wish to foul and the puppy encouraged to foul or urinate on the pad. The pad, or rather other pads of paper, are then moved nearer and nearer to the door leading to the outside garden, and the dog encouraged to continue to use the pad as a toilet area. Finally the pad arrives at the door and in the next day or so it is finally placed outside the door. When the puppy is found walking to the door, the owner must immediately allow the puppy outside to use the paper pad – and then *voilà* the dog is house-trained. Personally I find this a rather unnecessary piece of Skinnerian learning, for I have always house-trained puppies by putting them outside to evacuate their bowels and bladder as soon as they wake or have eaten. However many people swear by the paper pad method of house-training and I have seen many dogs successfully house-trained by it.

There are also certain proprietary brands of esters that, if sprinkled on the paper pad, will encourage the puppy to use it. These chemicals may replicate the scent of dog urine, and encourage the puppy to foul where another dog has apparently urinated. Gregarious species of wild canid certainly tend to overmark spots where others of the species have fouled, as lamp posts and fire hydrants in towns and villages attest. These chemicals emit odours which are usually only slightly detectable to the human olfactory senses, but are inviting to puppies and adult dogs alike – shades of Rabelais perhaps but nevertheless manufacturers claim their products hasten the house-training of puppies.

It should be of interest to the house-proud dog owner that puppies will usually become completely house-trained in a matter of two weeks if the owner is vigilant in observing when the puppy is about to urinate or defecate. Few dogs are naturally inclined to foul indoors. It is quite useless, and incidentally very counter-productive, to chastise a puppy that makes a mistake during the house-training programme, for it is unlikely that the puppy will see any connection between the fact that it has performed a perfectly normal bodily function and the beating it is receiving. Puppies are easily confused by the irrational behaviour of human beings and I am half-inclined to believe that Freud – who was often accused of having a lavatorial mind – was correct when he concluded that many of the peculiarities manifested by his patients were attributed to mistakes made during their early toilet-training.

It is, however, rather more difficult to toilet-train a young puppy if the owner is out of the house for most of the day.

It is in fact very difficult, and the owner must expect to return to find the puppy has often made a considerable mess of the room in which it has been left. Puppies so left seem to produce such an inordinately large quantity of urine that many newcomers to keeping dogs fear that their charges may be suffering from kidney disorders; and the fact that a whelp is seldom naturally discreet about where it deposits its faeces (and hence tramples filth around the room) often leads the uninitiated dog owner to believe it is 'unnaturally filthy'. To anyone who wishes to keep a dog yet must spend much of his or her day out of the house, I would advise paper-training the puppy – possibly encouraging it to use a pad of newspaper contained in a large low-sided waterproof tray. It is extremely difficult to toilet-train a puppy on a part-time basis, encouraging it to perform its bodily functions during the morning or evening, but leaving it to its own devices for the rest of the day. Many dog-owners arrange their annual holidays to coincide with the purchase of a puppy and subject the whelp to an intensive period of toilet-training before returning to work. I have never considered this to constitute a wasted holiday, the dog will no longer foul where it will, making the ownership of such an animal something more akin to a living nightmare than a pleasure.

In case the reader imagines that I have dealt too long with the process of house-training the puppy, or that I have an unwholesome interest in the bodily wastes of canids, it should be pointed out that many dogs are so badly house-trained that they have rendered their beloved owner's abodes foetid, unsightly, embarrassing hovels; and many dogs go to their graves bewildered as to why their owners experience distress when the dogs perform perfectly normal functions on expensive rugs and carpets and furniture.

I am only too aware just how many people become frantic when they fail to house-train a puppy and return the confused and now slightly maladjusted puppy to the breeder because 'the puppy won't house-train'. I have no statistics on just how many even more distraught owners finally have perfectly normal puppies 'put to sleep' because the house has become an evil-smelling hell, simply because of the owner's inability to house-train a young whelp. So I make no apology for the length of this chapter, for house-training is one of the most important aspects of training the family dog.

7

Training a Puppy to Come to Hand

The trouble-at-mill-type Yorkshire saying, 'There's nowt so queer as folk' is absolutely true – and if I might elaborate on the saying yet further I must add 'There's nowt more queer than folk who keep lurchers'. Lurchers are fast hunting dogs – composites of collies and greyhounds – bred, to use a cliché, 'to have speed, nose and sagacity', but such is the poor standard of training given to most lurchers that they soon become some of the biggest nuisances in the British countryside when they are let loose, free of their leashes. The sight and scent of huntable or coursable quarry invariably overrides any commands issued by their distraught and angry owners.

My 'Lurcher and Longdog' column in the sporting magazine *Shooting News* attracts a variety of unwanted guests to my home, all of whom claim to own the fastest lurcher – a somewhat dubious distinction, as no lurcher has the speed of a pure-bred greyhound. When faced with such a boast, and I confess my own lurchers are not fast dogs, I usually reply, 'How quickly does it come back when you call it?' which usually deflates the boaster like a pin in a rubber balloon. Just occasionally I get the reply, 'When he's ready, he'll come back' – a somewhat open-ended statement that bodes ill for any stock-keeper living within miles of a man claiming to own a speedy if recalcitrant lurcher. Nothing is more humiliating to a dog-owner than the smiles on the faces of onlookers who are watching him shout and yell to a dog to return to hand, while the dog totally ignores the command and runs on.

If I might liken the training of a dog to the progress of Pilgrim in Bunyan's book, the process of house-training a dog might be regarded as Pilgrim's initiation to the perils of the world, but the Slough of Despond, the point at which most dog-trainers fail dismally, is surely the training of a dog to come to hand instantly and without question. Many, many dog-owners are unable to let their wards off their leashes for fear that they will not come to hand once they have the opportunity to run off. The reader may be astonished to learn that certain dog-trainers in and around London make a good (if somewhat difficult) living by visiting owners of dogs that are reluctant to come to hand, and simply teaching the dog to return to its owner when called. Yet if one starts a training programme sensibly and proceeds in the same manner, most dogs can be taught to return to hand quickly and, what is most important, willingly.

Dogs are pure hedonists – they seek pleasure and avoid pain – and never is such a statement as easily proved as when a dog-breeder rears a litter of puppies and gives them a lot of attention from the time they are born until they leave the premises. Many six-week-old puppies will come instantly to hand when called; they will often know their names and answer if called. Puppies obtain great pleasure from being handled and fussed over and from being fed, and if the puppies are called by name to feed at separate feed trays it is amazing how well a small-time dog-breeder with time to spare for his whelps can get each one to respond when its name is uttered. I served my apprenticeship as a part-time kennel-lad with a springer spaniel breeder called Tom Evans, who not only had *avant garde* views on dog-training as early as the 1950s, but carried on a non-stop conversation with his puppies while he fed them or when he squatted on his haunches in the run and played with them. Each litter he bred was given precisely the same 'pet names' as the previous litter, and long before the litter was scheduled to leave for gundog-training each puppy would come instantly to hand once its name was called. Tom would enter the run where the puppies were housed with a set of small food dishes balanced on a baker's board. He would call Jack and as soon as Jack paid the slightest heed to the command his dish would be placed on the floor to allow him to feed. Likewise Jill, Taff and Socks – and each and every litter produced a puppy Tom insisted on calling Socks – would come to hand immediately their names were called.

Tom spent much time squatting on his haunches in the run, calling each puppy to him by name, and making almost absurd gestures of affection when it came to him. He was a tough, hardy man yet he displayed no inhibitions about demonstrating affection to the puppies he reared. He was in fact one of the great dog-trainers and I gained much from the time I spent at his tiny kennels in Blaengarw.

Training a puppy to come to hand should start on the day it arrives at its new home, but before training starts the owner should not only decide on the name the whelp is to be given, but should stick to the name for ever after. Many puppies are called by a succession of pet names before the owner finally decides on the name he intends to give it. This is totally confusing for the puppy, who is one day called Pepe and the next Gem, only to find that on the third day it is once again referred to as Pepe.

Some hours after the puppy has arrived and overcome possible travel sickness it will start to feel hungry and should be fed. Attract the puppy's attention to the dish, and as the dish is placed on the floor utter the name one intends to give the puppy, e.g. Jack. The chances are the puppy will associate the dish and the smell of its contents with food and come to hand immediately to be fed. The name Jack should be uttered as soon as the puppy starts to move towards the dish. Soon it will equate its name with feeding and come as soon as its name is uttered. Likewise the name Jack should be uttered and once the whelp has come to hand it should experience a show of effusive affection from the owner. Hence the dog associates the process of coming to hand when its name is called with some form of pleasure or reward – and it is extremely counter-productive to punish a recalcitrant dog if it comes instantly to its name, for it should never experience pain, fright or any sensation other than pleasure when it hears its name and comes readily to hand.

At one time I lived in Rotherham, where I used to watch the dog-owners exercising their dogs on the playing fields near my house and note the social interplay between man and dog. After a while I no longer became amazed at how badly most dogs were trained, but was increasingly surprised at how well most dogs behaved despite the illogical treatment they received from their owners. Many owners would shout desperate pleas for their dogs to return to hand, and then punish the dog when it did so. The dog of course failed to associate the beating it received with the naughty behaviour that had infuriated its owner some minutes before, but believed it was being beaten simply because it had decided to come to hand. More than once I observed a dog-owner, chain and leash concealed behind his back, coax and cajole a dog to return to him only to produce the leash and belabour the dog. The wretched animal must have been bewildered, but it is extremely difficult not to give vent to one's temper and punish a dog that has offended even when it comes to its name readily. It is also useless to justify one's actions by claiming 'He knows he's done wrong,' because the dog usually does not know he has. The dog genuinely believes he is being punished for coming to hand, and then acts accordingly next time he is called to return to his owner.

It is however very difficult to not lose one's temper or behave irrationally when dog misbehaves or fails to come instantly to hand, particularly if the dog misbehaves in public, humiliating the owner and incurring the mockery or derision of bystanders. More than once have I reacted irrationally towards a dog that displeased me – though as a salve to my pride I must add I realised my mistake as soon as I made it. In my early twenties I obtained a white German shepherd bitch, a granddaughter of one of the fountainheads of the breed, Champion Avon Prince of Alumvale. She was a delight to train, though as a baby showed no inclination to retrieve. I had time to spare one holiday – or, to be more precise, I was so impoverished I had no money to take me outside the district in which I lived – and so I trained the bitch to a very high level of obedience long before she was really old enough to be taught complex skills. She was, however, as precocious as I was vain, and took to the training like a duck to water. Each day I trained her on the playing fields in the centre of a large estate, and my vanity was gratified by the compliments I received from the residents.

However pride ever cometh before a fall. One day, in the middle of a strict training session, a puppy of roughly the same age as my bitch materialised from nowhere. After quivering with excitement, my bitch broke training, ran after the other puppy and proceeded to cavort and play for five minutes or so. I called to her and noticed my inability to get her to return to hand had caused smirks on the faces of the audience my training sessions usually attracted. This exacerbated my anger. Minutes later the bitch returned to hand and – mistake of mistakes – I slapped her, not hard but hard enough for me to vent my anger, and certainly hard enough for her to be hurt and confused. A week later she was still circling me, reluctant to come to hand lest she provoked a similar outburst from me.

Hindsight is all too easy, but what exactly should have been my response to the bitch that 'cut and run' during training? On reflection I should have pretended to ignore the disobedience, and accepted the fact that puppies of all breeds need to play if they are to develop normally. When she returned I should have greeted her joyfully, apparently delighted that she had at last decided to return. To slap her was a lamentable lapse from commonsense and I was now viewed by my audience as not only an incompetent dog-trainer unable to call a dog to hand, but a brutal lout who slapped a puppy when it did not return.

Puppies should never be turned loose in areas from which they can escape before they come to hand instantly and eagerly; and it is unwise to attempt one's first training sessions in open fields or areas that can afford a puppy an escape route, or at a time of day when one's presence might invite an audience. Not only will the presence of people induce a sense of humiliation in the trainer whose puppy does not perform as the trainer expects, but the presence of people (or, worse still, people with young children or young dogs) will often cause the puppy to 'break' ignoring the entreaties of the trainer and running to investigate the strangers that have suddenly appeared on the training ground.

A strange dog wandering on to the areas where recall training is about to be conducted will often cause bedlam – and some embarrassment to the dog trainer who is unused to the ways of young whelps. Few young puppies are steady in the presence of older dogs and the majority of free-running puppies will disregard the commands of the trainer and seek to investigate the other dog. One of two reactions are bound to occur, and both can be disconcerting to the novice trainer. If the other dog is a youngster or manifests the peculiarities of a young animal (and certain older dogs do have Peter Pan dispositions) the puppy will usually start to indulge in a wild game with the other dog, and will almost certainly ignore the commands and pleas of the trainer. If the other dog is an adult and displays even the slightest aggression, the youngster in training may panic and run screaming from the adult even though it has not attacked or apparently menaced it. Certain preludes to attack are all too obvious to a dog, but may be completely overlooked by a human being. Few normal adult dogs of any breed (and this includes even the most ferocious pit bull terriers) will attack a puppy without manifesting warning signs which alert a youngster to the danger. An adult dog often merely has to stare at a puppy to cause it to panic and run. Indeed staring is a prelude to attack in most species of animal and this has been noted by students of animal behaviour for centuries. Mowgli, the child adopted by wolves, the hero of Kipling's *The Jungle Book*, is asked to leave the wolf pack because his tendency to stare at his lupine brethren unnerves them. Young puppies are often terrified if they suddenly encounter the stare of a strange adult dog and such is the state of panic induced that the youngster may run screaming, tail between its legs, far from the trainer. Puppies who behave in such a manner seem for some reason to cause either great concern or great mirth among bystanders who are unaware of pack behaviour. To such uninitiated observers the sight of a puppy running screaming from an older dog (particularly if the puppy is larger than the adult) is an indication that the puppy is of craven disposition, for few people can resist crediting animals with human sentiments, values or emotions. In point of fact this apparently cowardly reaction has been noted amongst young wild canids when they encounter animals of the same species that are unfamiliar or from different packs. The flight of the youngster ensures its survival, for it is seldom pursued by the adult.

The trainer must be aware of these possible reactions to a strange dog and know how to bring the exuberant or terrified puppy to hand – and it is almost inevitable that he will be faced with the situations described at some stage of the puppy's training.

A young puppy engaged in a wild game with another dog should be allowed to run off its playfulness unless its cavorting places it in great danger – the pair are approaching a road for example. The most the trainer should do is to follow silently behind the pair until the excitement of the game is passed and then retrieve the puppy, making a display of pleasure when the puppy has returned, despite the fact that its apparent disobedience has infuriated him. Puppies so excited will often be a little shy at coming to hand possibly because they are still exhilarated by the game and possibly because they sense a feeling of animosity or anger from their owner – for many thousands of years of symbiosis between dog and man have given the dog a unique understanding of human moods.

I am faced with situations of this kind every time I attempt to train a puppy, as is every dog-trainer who cannot avail himself of a private paddock in which to train his dog, and I have devised a series of techniques to deal with puppies who are reluctant to come to call for such reasons. I find dropping onto one's hands and knees, so that one's face is level with that of the puppy, is efficacious in encouraging it to come to hand. There are many theories concerning why a puppy does come to hand when his owner assumes this position – though I certainly don't believe the popular notion that a stare from the human eye causes the puppy to be submissive and come to hand. My own theories are that either the puppy assumes that the trainer dropping to his hands and knees is assuming the play posture and therefore offers no threat whatsoever to the puppy or that the puppy is baffled by the trainer's change of shape, and comes to investigate what has caused the phenomenon. It is also likely that the action of towering over the puppy – and an adult human being must seem terribly large – intimidates the youngster and that 'coming down to the puppy's level' so to speak, is less frightening to the puppy that is contemplating returning to hand.

However some puppies, particularly puppies exhilarated by a game with another young dog, may still be a shade reluctant to come to hand, even though the trainer has dropped to his hands and knees. Reluctant puppies may circle the owner just out of reach of his hands, wagging their tails excitedly but still refusing to come to hand.

If the trainer suddenly turns his back on the puppy it may come to hand to investigate what has caused him to perform this feat, and this may enable the trainer to catch the whelp. Likewise, if the owner, still in the crouched position takes some keys or small stones from his pocket, drops them on the ground and pretends to take an earnest interest in them while ignoring the puppy, the whelp will usually come in close to investigate, and hence can be caught up. People viewing the spectacle, particularly ones who have never trained dogs, may regard the trainer as either a madman or a simpleton with a fascination for small stones. It is indeed difficult to maintain one's dignity while training a young puppy and those who are reluctant to appear slightly foolish at any time, should not obtain a puppy to train or never let it off the leash.

Once the puppy has decided to come to hand the trainer should avoid making any gesture that shows his displeasure, and should engage the whelp in a game before putting it back on the leash. Coming to hand should always be pleasurable for the puppy and nothing should be done to reduce this. Few whelps enjoy being put on the lead after a wild romp and so the return to hand must be buffered by an effusive display of affection. If the trainer immediately traps the puppy with a leash without an effusive display of affection, the whelp may well associate coming to hand with a reaction that it finds less than pleasant – and it will be more reluctant to come to hand next time it is allowed to run free.

I continue to lay emphasis on coming to hand until the dog is in its dotage partly because many of the dogs I keep and train are hunting dogs that need to be constantly under control, and partly because I get great pleasure from watching the faces of dog-owning friends when my dogs instantly return to hand as soon as I whisper their names or snap my fingers. When my dogs perform this feat I always reward them either by stroking, or scratching the pinna of their ears, or offering them a tiny titbit of food. Returning to hand on command must always be a pleasurable exercise for the dog. Furthermore I often exercise my dogs alongside flocks of Cheviot sheep, and I firmly believe I have the consent of the owners of the land simply because my dogs appear so obedient and return to hand with such alacrity. If the reader considers the pride I take in the obedience of my dogs to be ostentatious, so be it, and I will concede they have a point: however, in a world that is becoming increasingly hostile to badly behaved dogs, perhaps it is not unreasonable to convince landowners that one's dogs are under constant control. I call my lurchers to hand and fondle their ears as many as a score or more times a day, while they are out hunting, and the action obviously increases my affinity with them. I find the action pleasurable and so do my dogs.

Before discussing the subject of the leash and lead-training, it is perhaps expedient to remind the reader that some breeds of dog are decidedly reluctant to come to hand even as young puppies. Siberian huskies turned loose somewhere they are able to escape, will often do so rather than come to hand.

The majority of people who train these exquisite sled dogs are aware of their peculiarities and act accordingly. Newcomers to the breed may however be extremely disconcerted by the huskies' tendency to 'run on' rather than return to hand – and indeed there is much to be said for not allowing a Siberian husky to exercise in places where it is not easily caught up. It is true that there are people who train their animals to a high level of obedience and even win obedience awards with Siberian huskies; but it is equally true to say that many amateur trainers and first dog-owners are woefully out of their depth when they attempt to train these dogs. Such dogs may well have to be exercised on leashes for their entire lives – which brings us neatly on to the subject of lead-training.

8

Lead-Training

I must confess I don't enjoy lead-training a puppy, and I have often considered the process traumatic to both the dog and myself. I tend to feel exhausted and disenchanted after a lead-training session, and my disenchantment is exacerbated when I glance down and see a frightened puppy slavering at the mouth, with a bewildered look on its face. I always try to make the sessions as gentle as possible, so that they become less hurtful and upsetting to the puppy and to myself.

It is possible to take a puppy – even one from a breed such as some strains of working bearded collie that have a justly earned reputation for being lead-shy – fix it with a choke chain, indulge in a spectacle which rivals the Calgary Stampede, and have the puppy accepting, though absolutely loathing, the choke chain by the end of a very furious and thoroughly upsetting morning's training. Frankly I am reluctant to face such a labour, not only out of sympathy with the dog, but also because the exercise upsets me as much as it does the puppy, and the bond between puppy and man is weakened by such an epic struggle. Puppies so trained are reluctant to come to hand when their owners are carrying the dreaded choke chain, so while I feel it is virtually impossible to make lead-training pleasurable it is nevertheless possible to reduce the trauma – though I will concede that my methods often extend lead-training by several days.

When a puppy is restricted by a lead for the first time it will perform in one of two ways. Some puppies actively fight the lead, spinning round and round the trainer, screaming and bucking wildly to be rid of the loathsome device that is preventing them from doing exactly as they please. This type of puppy will often actively attack the restraining lead, sometimes leaving deep bite marks in the leather leash or sometimes chewing at the chain attachment with such fury as to cause its own gums to bleed. Such a puppy will cause some distress through its antics and attract antipathy to its handler from those who have never trained a dog – hence I would advise that all preliminary lead-training sessions be performed in private. Nevertheless the puppy that actively fights against the lead and hurls itself around like a demented fiend is usually fairly quickly lead-trained – though I must concede that I find the lead-training of such a whelp fairly distressing to watch.

A far more difficult puppy to lead-train is the one that does not actively resist the chain, but simply flops down on its belly, a terrified and bewildered look on its face, and simply refuses to move. It is almost impossible to predict how a puppy will behave when it is first restricted by a lead. Some of the most outgoing animals I have ever seen simply flopped down and refused to move when a lead was placed around their necks and their movements curtailed. One of the very worst offenders was a young lurcher bitch called Phaedra – a tenth-generation home-bred that was bred from a very biddable and easily trained family. Phaedra had wandered around at my heels for days before I attempted to lead-train her and I honestly believed her lead-training would be simplicity itself. I could not have been more wrong. When I placed the lead on her she simply fell on her side and refused to move. I stood over her for an hour attempting to coax her to her feet in order to begin the lead-training session but she refused to move and her eyes became glazed with terror when I tried to ease her to her feet. When I finally succeeded in getting her to stand she promptly toppled over again, and lay on her side, wetting herself in fear. I should like to be able to say that my experience with dogs generally, and this family of lurchers in particular, made me rather blasé about her actions. It would be a complete lie to say this. I was perplexed to say the least by the effect lead-training was having on the puppy, and I realised the bond that had developed between the puppy and myself was getting thinner by the minute.

Paradoxically, once Phaedra was free of the leash she stuck to my heels as if glued to them, and was as friendly and sycophantic as ever. Two hours later I once again attempted to lead-train her and she once again lay on her side as though petrified by the experience, her mouth held open, her eyes glazed with terror, and voiding faecal matter as she lay there. There are times when every normal dog-trainer who is not afflicted with an extreme form of megalomania encounters an animal that makes him doubt his own ability to train a dog to any standard, and this was one such time. I phoned friends who had been given Phaedra's litter-mates to enquire as to whether they too had experienced lead-training problems with their puppies, but it appeared that I was alone. Eventually I took to sitting on a pile of stones while Phaedra lay, paralysed by the effect of the leash, at my feet, and this process continued for a full week. At the end of the week the puppy condescended to stand while still on the leash and refrained from pulling against it. Very gingerly I arose from my pile of stones only to find Phaedra once more rolling on her back. I tried not to show my exasperation that bordered on despair, and once more sat on the stone pile. A day or so later Phaedra stood and remained standing while I gently raised myself from the stones and Phaedra trotted along at my heels as if she had always had a choke chain encircling her neck. I never again experienced the slightest problem with her and she grew into a very outgoing if slightly jealous sort of dog with no obvious psychological hang-ups. Curiously, she becomes ecstatic when she sees a leash as she knows it is an indication that she is to be taken hunting. Lest the reader should throw up his or her hands in despair at the description of this ordeal I should add that in many years of training I never once experienced comparable problems.

I should also add that it seldom takes longer than a day to lead-train most puppies.

At one time dogs were lead-trained in much the same manner as horses were halter-broken – that is they were tied in a loose box and allowed to lunge, buck and struggle to be free of the restricting leash, and only when they accepted that the leash could and would curtail their movements were they given formal lead-training. I'm sure this method works, but it must be extremely upsetting for the puppy.

I tend to favour more gentle methods of lead-training. When the puppy is deemed old enough to train I put a small light collar carefully but firmly around the puppy's neck and allow it to run free. For a while the whelp will usually attempt to snatch at or remove the collar from its neck, but within hours it will accept the presence of the collar. Some full-time breeders of gundogs allow a young puppy that has recently been collared to resume its place amongst its litter-mates with a length of rope attached to the collar. The theory behind this method of training is that it is only a matter of time before the puppy steps on the lead and thereby restricts its own movements, or the litter-mates tug at the rope hanging from the whelp's collar and thereby accustom it to the fact that it can be secured by the leash it is wearing. Many pointer and setter breeders swear by this method, which is simply an adaptation of the method often used to halter break foals; but the disadvantages of this method are, however, legion. Sooner or later the puppy will become frightfully entangled in the lead hanging from its collar.

I usually lead-train by attaching a strong lead to the puppy's collar and watching its reaction. If the puppy begins to buck and pull I am usually more pleased than I would be if it decided to flop down and refuse to move. If it bucks and rears I allow it to wind its way around me, turning my own legs and body to prevent a tangle. Eventually, and it doesn't usually take too long, the puppy, exhausted by its lunges, comes to terms with the fact that not only can it not escape from the leash, but that if it struggles, pulls, bucks or rears the sensations it experiences are decidedly unpleasant. It is a very stupid or extremely maladjusted dog that does not accept the restrictions imposed by a leash after it realises how unpleasant fighting against the leash can be.

The dog that flops down on its belly, rolls on its back or side, and refuses to move needs a somewhat different approach. Pulling or yanking the whelp to its feet, or dragging it along the ground until it decides to co-operate, is a counterproductive technique, for it results in the puppy becoming disturbed or unwilling to come to hand. The flopper, as such a puppy is often referred to in dog-training circles, should be treated with care and if possible coaxed to its feet by offering titbits (though most floppers are so terrified by their first contact with the leash that they will refuse to eat while tethered).

There are several ways of getting a puppy that has flopped back on its feet and walking on the lead. Firstly, if the leash is extended with a length of rope and the trainer, still holding the rope, walks some twelve feet from the puppy, crouches (the reader may remember how readily the puppy will come to someone who has crouched) and calls the puppy to hand, the chances are the puppy will rise to its feet and walk to the owner. If the puppy will accept a reward in the form of some food it enjoys, then by all means feed it when it comes to hand. If the puppy will not, make a fuss of it – though the chances are that the flopper is so traumatised by its first experience with the leash it may look extremely forlorn when it comes to hand. Sooner or later the whelp will become accustomed to the leash and will accept that flopping does not bring an end to the training programme.

There is yet another dodge that can be employed to lead-train a persistent 'flopper'. If the flopper is accustomed to playing with another dog, preferably a puppy of roughly the same age or if not, at least a dog with which it has a good relationship, then the other dog – which of course must be lead-trained – can be walked ahead of the flopper and with luck the flopper will rise and attempt to follow its playmate. Puppies which are persistent floppers, or which manifest other peculiarities, will usually train fairly easily if their dams are walked in front of them.

Lead-training is often tedious and tiring, but it is of such importance that the would-be dog-trainer must master the exercise if the puppy is to proceed further in its training programme. At this point it is perhaps expedient to discuss the three principal types of dog leashes: namely the collar and lead; the choke chain; and that newcomer to dog training devices, the Halti.

For many centuries the collar and leather or chain lead were the only means of leading the dog where the owner required it to go, and many museums exhibit primitive dog collars which are little different from the ones manufactured today. The prick-eared pet dog depicted on the floor of the private house in Pompeii is wearing a collar and lead similar to those sold on stalls at Kennel Club and country shows. Likewise the popular Romano-British goblets manufactured at Gloucester are decorated with designs showing a very puzzled-looking fallow deer being chased by a greyhound that is wearing a leather-type collar. Taplin's ferocious-looking mastiffs and greyhounds shown in that much-quoted book *The Sportsman's Cabinet* (1803) are also restrained by dint of heavy chains and leather collars.

Thus when the choke chain made its appearance amongst the dog-training fraternity it is not surprising that purists rejected this running loop of chain as cruel and barbaric. For a while I confess I too found the choke chain (the very name implies savage cruelty) an anathema and only in my early twenties did I come to appreciate its value over the traditional leather collar as an aid to lead-training a puppy. For a leather collar to be of any use in restraining a bucking, rolling and struggling puppy without it slipping over the whelp's head it must be fitted a shade too tightly for comfort.

If the object of any type of collar-like device is simply to assure the puppy that when it has a collar and lead on there is simply no escape no matter how it bucks, rears, and pulls, then the choke chain, if fitted properly, is ideal. Furthermore, few puppies from the most timid to the most bold fail to realise that should they decide to pull either forwards or backwards the choke chain makes their antics less than comfortable. Yet it is surprising how many first-time dog-trainers fail to utilise the good qualities of the choke chain and simply use it as a rather inefficient garrotte that draws gasps from the recalcitrant dog or renders the timid dog more timid yet. If the choke chain is fitted properly and used correctly lead-training a dog becomes much easier for the beginner.

A choke is simply a length of galvanised chain that acts like a running noose. If the chain becomes damaged or corroded so that its function resembles that of the now illegal self-lock snare, then the choke chain becomes simply an instrument of torture. If fitted properly, a smooth, rust-free chain tightens on the dog's throat if it attempts to pull, throw itself around, or drag behind – and immediately the dog ceases to struggle the chain slackens and the discomfort ceases. It is a training aid that would delight a Pavlov: pulling or dragging behind equals pain; walking alongside the trainer equals the cessation of pain – but only if the chain is properly fitted.

During one of the frequent stormy periods in my teaching career – desperate times when I stacked corned beef, boxed middle-weight and delivered divorce writs rather than continue in teaching – I was heading for an inevitable clash with the Head for whom I worked which would equally inevitably result in my dismissal; I decided that I would prepare myself for the day by taking on recalcitrant dogs for training. Eventually I was to graduate and specialise in the training of disobedient sight hounds (and few dogs can be as badly trained as sight hounds) but in the early days my advertisement read 'All breeds taken for training'. The advert was made to look more ridiculous still by the fact that to drum up a little extra trade, and to fill the space for which I had paid, I added 'Latin, Greek and Hebrew translated'.

However, absurd as my advertisement must have appeared, it brought me two clients – one a would-be lurcher-trainer and the other the most inept yet amusing dog-trainer I have ever met. My phone rang and an incredibly breathless lady panted, 'Do you train Newfoundlands? I'm just about desperate.' I answered 'Yes, of course I do', even though my only contact with the breed was that at the age of eleven I had read Robert Michael Ballantyne's *The Dog Crusoe*, which curiously enough had started me on my path to training animals. 'Yes,' I repeated, feeling more competent by the minute. 'I'll be there in half an hour,' said the lady, still breathless.

Two hours later, when I had decided the advertisement was a bit of a waste of time and would have read better if I had omitted the statement concerning dog-training, a taxi arrived, the door opened and a huge brown dog tumbled out, panting madly and pulling with him a rather plump, dishevelled lady. She hung on to the leash for dear life as the dog towed her round the taxi while she attempted to pay off the amused driver.

The Newfoundland, an obese animal that would later manifest acute hip dysplasia, lunged towards me and the lady followed in hot pursuit. I observed that the choke chain, which fitted none too snugly around the dog's neck, had both eyes attached to the lead clip, which was subjected to such strain that it spoke highly of the technology of Taiwan. She had little need to explain her predicament, for the vision of a huge dog towing a somewhat small, dumpy lady explained all.

'The choke chain isn't fitted properly,' I explained gently, and rather less gently I grabbed the large, slobbering brute by the scruff of the neck while I re-threaded the chain. 'I've tried it like that but it chokes him', the lady countered. 'It's supposed to choke him if he pulls,' I replied, as the dog ran the length of his leash and jerked so hard that it practically pulled me off my feet. The ritual of getting a huge, powerful, rather silly dog to accept the limitations imposed by the choke chain took an exhausting twenty minutes – though it was clearly a source of great entertainment to the taxi driver who stayed to watch the spectacle.

However, an hour later, the flustered lady – almost as breathless as before – was walking a somewhat more

Left: Despite bad publicity, the German shepherd dog is usually versatile and easily trained with a sound temperament. The key to the German shepherd dog's behaviour lies with the trainer/owner.

Right: Malemutes, a strain of the Husky, are powerful dogs that are seldom easy to control.

Left: The St Bernard is all too prone to the ailments that are common amongst the 'giant' breeds.

Below: These wolf dog hybrids were the result of a German shepherd dog bitch mating with a Canadian timber wolf.

Although rescued dogs are endearing and difficult to resist, dog owners are warned of the dangers they may be risking when choosing one with no breeding history.

The rottweiler – a dog with an unjustifiably bad name.

Lead-training can be tiresome and frustrating, but once your dog obeys instinctively the rewards are well worth the effort.

This photograph illustrates the great importance of breaking all dogs (town and country) to stock.

Training a dog in the sit and down positions

Left: A lurcher held at the sit position.

Below: A lurcher dropped to the down position.

Above: A lurcher held at the down position.

Right: The trainer/owner backs away from the lurcher in the down position to test the dog's obedience level.

Retrieving training

Top, left to right: (i) The trainer/owner throws the object to be retrieved. (ii) The dog is commanded to retrieve the object. (iii) The dog picks up the scent of the object. *Above:* (iv) The well-trained dog will bring the object straight back to the trainer/owner. *Right:* (v) When the dog has carried out the sequence correctly, and obediently returns the object to the trainer/owner's hand, a great show of praise and affection is essential.

restrained and docile Newfoundland along my lane and was clearly amazed at the transformation the correct use of the choke chain had wrought. She thanked me profusely, paid me what I considered to be an extremely large sum (I was later to discover that, compared to the sum asked by full-time trainers, the amount I was paid was anything but excessive) and departed uttering such eulogies that I felt like a somewhat more forceful St Francis of Assisi.

I had much for which I could thank the lady, for through her auspices I was sent my first Afghan hound to train, and subsequently I specialised in training sight hounds. However, it seems that none of my tales are destined to have happy endings. Six months later, while travelling through Birmingham, I observed my breathless lady being towed around the Bull Ring by her Newfoundland. She had once more reverted to the habit of attaching both eyes of the choke chain to the lead clip.

Big, powerful dogs left too long without being trained are invariably lead-broken by the use of a choke chain. The chain, when properly set and jerked sharply, is able to restrain the rowdiest and most boisterous dog instantly and to subdue the most wilful dog in far less time than if a dog is lead-broken by dint of the conventional collar and lead. However, to use the choke chain as a type of garrotte to throttle a dog into submission is one of the most brutal and counter-productive training methods imaginable, and I have seen choke chains pulled so hard that they damaged both the larynx and vertebrae of the dog. The choke chain should be jerked to restrain the dog, but the pressure around the dog's throat should be slackened as soon as the dog complies with the trainer's wishes.

In recent years behaviourists and animal psychologists have done much to improve the devices and appliances that the trainer can use to control over-exuberant dogs. One such appliance is the dream child of Dr Roger Mugford, a behaviourist who specialises in the modification of aberrant behaviour manifested by dogs and other mammals. The reader might well wish to read Mugford's excellent and lucid paper arguing that pit bull terriers that have engaged in pit battles with other dogs, fail to rehabilitate to a normal lifestyle in the company of dogs of any other breed. However, to return to the subject of lead-training particularly headstrong dogs, Mugford – who obviously had made a study of dynamics as well as animal behaviour – designed a series of head-straps which fit over the muzzle and head of the dog, thereby offering a fastening point for a leash. The Halti, as Mugford called the device he later was to patent, obviously bears a resemblance to the halter used on horses. Mugford does in fact believe that some dogs will pull, no matter how they are trained, and will often damage themselves or even their owners by doing so. In the early 1900s whippet trainers encouraged their wards to pull on the leash so that the dogs developed strongly muscled hind legs (the same training is incidentally given to pit bull terriers that are to be used for the illegal sport of dog-fighting). A Black Country newspaper cartoon of the early part of the century depicts a man with one massively developed arm while the other arm appears positively emaciated. The doctor treating this deformity is saying. 'Use the other arm more, lad – or else give up bloody whippet training.'

However, not everyone wishes to develop massive biceps by exercising a dog with a strong desire to pull, and Mugford remarks that the action of jerking the choke chain to restrain the dog has caused damage to the cartilaginous spinal discs in both dogs and their owners. Mugford is of the opinion that the choke chain is a cruel device (his opinion caused a storm amongst the dog-training fraternity when he first published his theories) and states that the Halti reduces the effort of walking dogs that have a tendency to pull. He states that 'the 100kg tow of a St Bernard was reduced to 2kg by using the Halti'.

At first the Halti had a mixed, even unfavourable reception amongst the dog fraternity. The device looks a shade unusual – until one is accustomed to seeing it in use, the Halti appears to resemble an instrument of torture rather than a device to aid the training of a large and powerful dog. I must confess that I was most reluctant to consider its use until 1990 when I saw a small, rather frail lady purchase a grown malemute – one of the most powerful dogs in the world. The dog had not been lead-trained, yet by using Mugford's patent, she was able to control this large and powerful dog in a manner that would have been impossible if she had resorted to a conventional collar and lead, and extremely difficult had she decided to lead-train the dog by dint of a choke chain.

While it would be a lie to say that I am now a convert to Mugford's extraordinary device – I still find the Halti an incongruous looking affair – it would also be a lie to say that the inventor of the Halti has not achieved great success. It has proven a boon to anyone who wishes to train an adult large, unruly dog.

9

Stock-Breaking

My present home is on the tourist route from Thurso to John o' Groats, a road that bristles with bed-and-breakfast houses and novelty shops selling intricately patterned home-made souvenirs, and even more intricately patterned glass ornaments. Every year brightly coloured, newly painted house-signs appear along the route, and every year signs warning the tourist about the dangers allowing dogs to run on land where sheep are grazing are erected. The farming fraternity must breathe a sigh of relief when the last camera-toting dog-owning tourist returns south. The county survives by catering for tourists and visitors are its life's blood, but dog-owning visitors often cause havoc amongst the flocks of Northern Cheviot sheep that provide the main income of the farmers and crofters of the county.

It would astound the reader if he could see the damage that even a small toy breed can perpetrate on a whole flock of sheep during a single hour of havoc. Sheep are in some ways the architects of their own destruction, and panic, rather than actual bites, cause most of the damage when a flock is pursued by a dog. There is a tale told in Sutherland of a tourist family who came north, bringing with them a King Charles spaniel – seemingly one of the more innocuous dogs imaginable. The dog escaped from the owners' camper van and simply chased the sheep around the pastures without inflicting a single bite on the hapless beasts – which nevertheless tumbled into ditches, breaking legs and necks in the process. Only three of the flock of fifty ewes and half-grown lambs survived the onslaught. The cost of the damage was astronomical and it is unlikely that those tourists will ever forget their Highland holiday, nor will the crofter who experienced the damage wrought by this tiny dog.

Few owners of pet dogs would believe that their beloved pets could even consider stock-worrying, but the truth is that the reactions of dogs allowed to run free in the countryside are very similar to those of truly wild canids – like Mary O'Grady and the Colonel's lady they are indeed 'sisters under the skin'. When livestock stands its ground and refuses to retreat as a dog approaches, the possibility of the dog following up with an attack is, to say the least, slight; but when livestock flees in panic before a dog the action awakens dark atavistic memories within the dog, and in a trice it has cast off the many thousand years of domestication and is once more the hunter of the savannah, pursuing its prey in deadly earnest. This metamorphosis is not only frightening for the dog owner to watch, but the veneer of civilisation is sloughed off so rapidly that the owner of an untrained pet dog is often unable to understand or predict the transformation. Few books ever deal with the subject of stock-worrying, or even acknowledge stock-worrying dogs exist; many seem to pretend that the carnage wrought by a stock-worrying pet dog is something that will never happen to the reader's animal. The truth is that if a dog is not broken to stock, the dog – any dog of any breed or cross-bred – is a potential stock-worrier. The new agricultural revolution is now providing recreational facilities rather than crops for the town-dweller – and with that town-dweller comes the town-dweller's dog – and make no bones about it, all dogs have the potential for being stock-worriers.

In his superb if rather savage book, *Dog Training*, Konrad Most is not far short of the mark when he suggests that all dogs are basically cowardly. This is borne out by the fact that the victims of the recent spate of dog attacks have usually been small, easily intimidated children, or people who displayed some fear in the presence of the dog, thereby encouraging it to attack them. Thus the fright of an animal in front of a dog accentuates the dog's desire to chase it, and the more nervous or prone to panic the victim may be, the more likely the dog is to push home its advantage. Just observe the day-to-day conflicts that occur on a typical cat-and-dog-riddled estate. Dogs will chase cats with great enthusiasm and may even hurt or kill a fleeing cat. However, should the self-same dog come across a Rum Tum Tugger straight out of the pages of *Possum's Book of Practical Cats* – a cat that stands its ground, lies in wait or even stalks the approaching dog – it will manifest somewhat different reactions. As soon as it sees the cat, the most persistent cat-chaser will pull and tug at its chain or leash, but as the dog approaches the immobile or obviously hostile cat – like an Etruscan forced into conflict on Horatius' bridge – its courage begins to fail and its lunges towards the cat become less furious. If the cat not only stands its ground but approaches the menacing dog, the dog may start to bark frantically; if the trainer listens carefully he will observe the tenor of the barking changes if the dog is brought nearer to the obviously unafraid cat as bravado and hostility is replaced by fear of the cat that refuses to run.

Hence creatures that are prone to panic or run are the most likely to be attacked by a pet dog. If the reader chooses to disbelieve this statement I suggest he or she investigates how few urban foxes are set upon by wandering dogs, and how many of the tiny water deer that are unwisely encroaching on the towns are chased and attacked by the most unlikely breeds of dog. Certain species of livestock are more likely to be attacked by dogs than others, and nothing seems to incur the fury of an otherwise docile house pet more than ducks. Ducks become not only hysterical but extremely vocal when approached by dogs, and their blind panic can trigger off the latent hunting instinct of most dogs that are not completely stock steady with ducks. Muscovy ducks, it can be argued, seldom run before a curious dog, but it can also be argued that Muscovy ducks are closely related to geese and geese have the happy knack of putting most dogs to flight. True ducks will panic, squawk, quack loudly and become a mass of hysterical feathers when a dog approaches, so dog owners need to pay particular attention to breaking dogs to domesticated ducks or similar species.

During my twenty-three years of hunting a pack of ratting terriers I worked my team of between thirty and sixty terriers amongst pigs, chickens, calves and horses, but I was always reluctant to allow my pack to hunt rat in sheds that housed ducks despite the fact that ducks attract large quantities of rats (which, curiously, will attack ducklings with a greater fury than they attack chickens of a comparable age). Furthermore, at the risk of appearing like the author of a book concerned with livestock management, ducks that have been frightened, let alone mauled, experience great trauma. Laying ducks such as the ubiquitous Khaki Campbells and Runner ducks promptly stop laying and start to moult when upset. Table ducklings such as Aylesburys and Pekins tend to stop growing while continuing to eat inordinate amounts of food if a dog so much as startles them. Lest the reader should feel this subject is out of place in a book concerned with dog-training, he or she may feel differently when an irate duck keeper presents an enormous bill for the damages wrought by a dog that has merely chased a small flock of ducks.

Victorian dog-trainers – often called dog-breakers, for obvious reasons – often used dramatic methods to break poultry-killing dogs of the habit. A popular method, used by Vero Shaw, was to allow the dog to kill a fowl and then hang it round the dog's neck until it rotted away or became one of those skin-covered skeletons so beloved of Hammer horror films. The theory was that the dog would become so sick of the putrid cadaver hanging round its neck that ever after it would fight shy of killing chickens or ducks. It is a fine method I suppose – except for the fact it doesn't work, and while I am fairly tolerant of stenches I do fight shy of training or working with a dog that has a putrefying hen hanging around its neck. Once an animal starts to putrefy or change its smell a dog will usually fail to recognise to which species the cadaver belongs and furthermore the dog's propensity to eat carrion would ensure that once the fowl began to decay the dog would set about devouring the carcass.

However for the most ludicrous and barbarous advice regarding breaking dogs to fowl, one would find it hard to beat the method advocated by Barbara Woodhouse in her book *Training Dogs My Way*, which is just about the tops in bizarre nonsense – and is a shade hard on fowls as well: Woodhouse recommends taking a confirmed fowl-chaser to a chicken pen, removing one of the fowls, chopping off its head, and then allowing the dog – which is attached to a choke chain – to chase the decapitated fowl around the yard, yanking the choke chain at the appropriate moment. If such a method had been suggested by a Haitian witch doctor, the public would have laughed and referred to the method as ludicrous ju-ju – as indeed it is. It would be interesting to know just how normal, sensitive people are supposed to steel themselves to perpetrate such an atrocity. For twenty-three years I hunted a pack of some of the gamest terriers in Britain amongst battery fowl, and if one of my helpers had suggested I used such a method I would have taken steps to have the man sent to see a doctor. There is no rhyme, reason or commonsense in such barbarous methods – and God knows how many people have been misguided and revolted by such ludicrous hocus-pocus.

Tom Evans of Blaengarw used a different, far more humane method. With the dog on a running leash he would not only yank the lead when the dog approached a sheep or fowl but fire a very noisy blank-firing pistol at the same moment. The noise terrified the dog at the very moment when the dog was expecting to experience great pleasure as it grabbed hold of the sheep or fowl. The method served two purposes – it broke every sheep-worrying dog that Tom was sent and terrified me so much that I repeatedly failed my marksman's test during my military service.

Cats are the most commonly chased type of livestock, partly because cats almost invariably run before the dog, and partly because it is the species that the urban dog-owner and his pet is most likely to encounter. Yet the cat is perhaps the most dangerous animal for the dog to pursue. Not only do they retaliate with great ferocity, and somehow managing to find the eyes of an attacker with their claws, but when chased they often dart in front of traffic and survive, whereas the pursuing dog may be somewhat less successful at negotiating a crowded road. When I lived in Rotherham during the 1960s there was a notorious stretch known as Meadow Bank Road, where scarcely a week went by without some luckless dog coming to grief while pursuing cats.

Sheep, however, are the livestock that urban-reared dogs are most likely to encounter on a trip to the country, and because sheep tend to run when they catch sight of a dog (in the light of my previous observations sheep have every reason to run), they are the most frequently damaged creatures when a dog escapes from its owner and runs riot in the countryside. Sheep-worrying attracts a great deal of publicity: lambs being torn to pieces by dogs is an emotive subject to say the least – even though those who are horrified by the thought will sit down to eat similar lambs later in the year. Furthermore, ewes are currently valued between £60 and £100 each by farmers, and young lambs at perhaps £40, thus the destruction of a flock by a dog can cost its owner a substantial amount of money.

So, having dealt – perhaps all too thoroughly – with the subject of livestock-worrying, how should the owner of a puppy train it so that it ignores, or at least is unlikely to chase, livestock.

It is extremely difficult to break a livestock-killer of the habit once the dog has experienced the pleasure of chasing, catching and possibly killing another animal – in view of which one must commend the greyhound rehabilitation societies which do such an excellent job rehabilitating track and coursing greyhounds so as to fill the role of a family pet. The art of stock-breaking a puppy simply consists of ensuring that the puppy is never allowed to chase livestock and has no desire to do so.

As soon as my puppies are inoculated and safe to take off

the premises they are walked on a leash amongst sheep. When a puppy is at the age 'when all was tall for I was small,' it is usually intimidated when livestock towers over it (the reader may remember that the puppy may well be intimidated when its owner towers over it) and seldom considers chasing the livestock. Chickens, particularly large and fairly aggressive cock birds, can be absolutely terrifying to a puppy and thus the whelp should be taken to see such stock – on a leash of course, lest it chase the poultry or sheep or, more than likely, run off to escape the beasts amongst which it is being walked. A puppy subjected to this form of training from the time it leaves the nest or is lead-trained seldom shows an interest in chasing stock when it is older. Should the puppy show the slightest interest in chasing livestock or engaging the livestock in play – which will eventually lead to stock-chasing – a jerk on the lead and the word 'no' uttered forcefully will usually restrain it.

It is worth noting that the word 'puppy' is being used in the singular, for it is absolute lunacy to attempt to stock-break two puppies simultaneously, particularly if one is dealing with one of the more aggressive breeds such as terriers. The presence of another puppy at a stock-breaking session gives extra courage to each whelp and hence they are far less intimidated by the presence of larger animals such as sheep or poultry. One puppy may well shy away or cower when a sheep or a cockerel approaches it, but two or more puppies will usually bark at or attempt to chase the stock to which they are being broken. Sir Jocelyn Lucas once remarked that in the presence of another dog a puppy's courage increases tenfold – so to take along another puppy or, worse still, an unbroken older dog, is to court disaster.

A puppy should be stock-broken to ducks with the utmost care for the reasons just explained, and if it shows the slightest interest in chasing the ducks or engaging them in some sort of game, it must be checked by dint of a sharp pull of the lead. Only when a puppy shows a disinclination to chase stock of any kind, or indifference in the presence of stock, should it be allowed off the lead in the presence of animals that are likely to run and thereby incite the puppy to chase them. It is in fact far easier to stock-break a puppy than to cure the vice of chasing stock once it has developed.

Personally, I dread taking out my dogs in sheep country if another dog that is an unknown quantity is present. Sheep- and poultry-chasing is terribly infectious, and if a hitherto steady dog is subjected to the sight of another dog chasing sheep it may well become very much less steady on future occasions. I dislike taking packs of dogs anywhere, for that matter – particularly if I have not trained them myself or have personal knowledge of the way they behave with livestock. Somewhere someone is surely compiling a book of epic proportions, entitled *Famous Last Words*, and a goodly sized chapter of the said tome is surely entitled 'Yes, I'm sure he'll be fine with sheep.'

I always keep an eye on trained dogs when I am taking them through sheep country and if I am a shade oversensitive concerning sheep the reader must forgive me. I was born in a Welsh mining valley where sheep crowded the streets and foraged in trash cans for potato peelings; and over the years I have had many dogs sent to me to cure them of sheep-worrying.

The laws regarding dogs worrying sheep are fairly explicit and easily interpreted even by the layman. Under Section 1 of the Protection of Livestock Act 1953 the owner of a dog or – if the owner is not in charge of the dog at the time – both the owner and the handler are committing offences if the dog worries livestock on agricultural land. Under the Act cattle, sheep, goats, pigs, horses, asses, mules, and all sorts of domestic fowl are considered livestock, though game is not protected under this Act.

The protection livestock receive under the 1981 Wild Life and Countryside Act is rather more far reaching, for it extends the definition of worrying to include situations in which the dog is not actually chasing the sheep but wandering at large where sheep are pastured. If the dog is not under close control in these conditions – either on a leash, or a yard or so from the owner – the owner or handler may be guilty of an offence.

Where injury to stock or loss of stock has been incurred a magistrate may award compensation, but even if the dog owner escapes conviction, the owner of the livestock that has been damaged or killed may pursue a civil action to recover any money he may consider that he has lost through the actions of an unruly or stock-worrying dog.

The Animals Act of 1971, which was prompted by a spate of stock-worrying that occurred in the late 1960s, is a civil law that provides a means whereby owners of livestock that are troubled by unruly dogs can secure compensation for damage done. Tame or domesticated deer, and pigeons, pheasants, partridges and quails prior to their release were added to the list of animals covered by the 1953 Protection of Livestock Act. There are instances of enraged landowners seeking redress against dog-owners who allowed dogs to bark at cattle, thereby stampeding them into barbed wire; and at least two successful prosecutions agains dog-owners who allowed a dog to bark at poultry and caused the hens which were frightened by the din to go 'off lay'.

The Animals Act of 1971 also provides for owners of livestock to shoot and kill a dog that is in the process of killing or harming livestock if the dog cannot be restrained by any other means. The police must be informed within forty-eight hours of the killing of the dog.

I make no excuse for this somewhat lengthy digression concerning the legal rights of landowners and the legal responsibilities of dog-owners when their dogs upset, hurt or kill livestock. Many dog-owners are ignorant of their responsibilities, and they should be made aware of the problems an unruly dog can create in the countryside, and the enormous sums of money such a dog can cost its owner.

A persistent sheep-worrier is hard to break of its habit, particularly if its owner or handler wishes to avoid committing acts of cruelty that might well bring down prosecutions under the far-reaching ramifications of the Protection of Animals Act of 1911. Section 1 (i)(a) of the Act makes it an offence to cruelly beat, kick, ill-treat, over-ride, over-drive, torture, infuriate or terrify any animal, or to cause the animal any unnecessary suffering by wantonly or unreasonably doing or omitting to do any act (failing to treat injuries or infections, etc). The infliction of pain for a necessary purpose may not be considered as a cruel act, but unnecessary or unreasonable abuse of the animal may amount to cruelty. This shadowy or grey area of the law leads us quite neatly back to the subject of how a confirmed sheep- or poultry-worrier might be broken of its injurious and often extremely costly habit.

Some of the old and tried methods of breaking stock-worrying dogs certainly contravene the Protection of Animals Act 1911, even though they are highly effective. One such method was to take a twelve-yard length of some extremely strong rope or chain, and attach the persistent sheep-worrier to a ram belonging to some rather primitive type of sheep. Black-face rams or even the diminutive but fiery Shetland rams were considered the very best breeds to use for this purpose, though Welsh mountain rams were also very able and willing to defend themselves against the most ferocious dogs. The spectacle that followed attaching the dog to the ram often resembled a duel from one of the early science fiction tales by Edgar Rice Burroughs, for whereas the ram could not escape from the dog, neither could the dog escape the attentions of the enraged ram. At first the more persistent dog might well have taken the battle to the ram, only to be met by a set of sharp horns and a skull nearly half an inch thick – and few dogs would be standing after being charged by a ram. A dog that had been winded and dazed by the impact would either renew its attack, or what is more likely, attempt to escape the attentions of the mass of bone and horn that was attacking it. Should the dog renew the attack, the ram would be more than willing to follow up its initial warning shot; should the dog attempt to escape, the leash would pull the ram towards the dog and this would usually prompt another attack from the ram. In a matter of minutes, the implacable hatred the sheep-worrier manifested towards sheep would be replaced by a terror of the species it once delighted in chasing. An hour of this treatment would usually reduce the most persistent sheep-worrier to a cowering pathetic creature, with little taste for further adventures with sheep.

At the risk of offending the reader with a macabre anecdote, I must add that this method of stock-breaking is not always as efficacious as it would appear. In 1948 I witnessed a bull terrier – a persistent sheep-worrier of the first order – which had been tied to a Welsh Mountain ram and invited to do its worst. An hour later the antagonists were still facing each other: the dog's ribs pulverised by the furious pounding given it by the ram, and the ram's ears chewed down to the head. The dog was speckled with blood but still defiant, if bewildered by what it had been forced to endure. I have little doubt that this bizarre and extreme method would have meant prosecution under Section 1 (i)(a) of the Protection of Animals Act 1911, though in the light of the dog's reputation as a sheep-worrier, a solicitor for the defence might have argued that the pain inflicted was for a 'necessary purpose'.

Likewise a ewe with a new-born lamb may well attack a dog to protect her offspring, and the most valiant defenders of their lambs are perhaps Welsh Mountain ewes. Despite the fact that these ewes are not horned, the impact of a solidly constructed and bony skull on the head and body of most breeds of dog will usually deter the most enthusiastic sheep-chasers. Yet, once again, it should be mentioned that while the infliction of pain upon the dog is for a necessary purpose – to deter it from sheep-worrying – the unreasonable abuse of either animal may well amount to cruelty for even if the ewe attacked the dog to defend her lambs, there is little doubt that she would be terrified by the encounter with a hostile dog.

Efficacious these methods may be but they invite prosecution by their very nature. I am also sure that Hollingsworth's suggestion that a chicken-worrying dog would be cured of its problems by allowing it to be attacked by an Asil game cock bird would not only be efficacious but would also certainly invite prosecution under the Protection of Animals Act 1911 Section 1 (i)a. Atkinson has described the fury and power of such birds in his books concerning the illegal sport, cock-fighting. He tells of an Asil cock bird that attacked him, he managed to duck the cock bird's spurs – the natural horny spurs, quite distinct from the metal spikes that are fixed to the heels of English game cocks – pierced a door so deeply that the bird needed to be freed by prising its spurs from the wood with metal pliers. Stuart Cloete records that such cock birds were kept by Boer farmers to protect other fowl from attack by hawks and small mammalian predators, but while it is true a dog might be seriously injured by a wound from such a spur, a persistent chicken-worrier might well snap at and kill such a bird with a single bite – and this would exacerbate rather than curb the dog's enthusiasm for chicken-worrying.

More acceptable methods therefore need to be considered if the dog-handler is to stay well clear of committing offences or being accused of perpetrating acts of unnecessary cruelty to animals. A persistent sheep-worrier should be fastened with a check line – a line twelve to twenty yards long that is constructed of material that will resist the sudden lunges of a dog – and taken to a spot where sheep or poultry can be encountered. If the dog shows any desire to chase the stock the check line should be yanked and the word 'no' uttered sharply. The handler must learn to gauge the most suitable length and weight of line for the particular dog, so that the sharp yanking action has the greatest effect in deterring the dog. I find that a dog wearing a choke chain rather than a conventional collar learns the error of its ways more quickly when worked on a check line. This method does not of course offer the instant cure that a battering by a ram or an attack by an enraged Asil cock bird might, and the trainer using a check line may need to take several weeks to ensure the dog is stock-steady in the countryside.

Not all livestock tends to turn and run before a dog. A gamekeeper, writing for one of the sporting periodicals in the 1980s, mentions that his fields were plagued by poachers who caught hares, rabbits and pheasants with lurchers and longdogs (composite sight hounds specifically created to catch hare and deer). His problems came to an end when the landowner leased the field to some owners of ponies and bullocks which, disturbed by a beam of light shining around the field, actively attacked the dog that was chasing the rabbits illuminated by the light. It is a fact that many lurchers that have been scared out of their wits by horses and bullocks – and young stallions are often particularly aggressive to dogs that trespass on land they consider to be their domains – are often found wandering in the fields after a poaching foray has been interrupted by hostile or curious livestock. I make a point of instantly calling my dogs to hand and leashing them up when I find bullocks or horses approaching the dogs. A panic-stricken dog running away from apparently hostile livestock can be as big a nuisance as a dog that actively chases the livestock. Dogs that are leashed when bullocks start to encircle them are seldom as terrified as they would be if they were allowed to run free.

It should now be obvious that the correct time to stock-break a dog is when it is young enough to be intimidated by livestock. If the dog is allowed to get older and more confident before it is introduced to livestock the task of breaking it becomes more difficult; if the dog is allowed an opportunity to chase livestock the task of ameliorating its behaviour becomes more difficult still. Dogs which have killed sheep or poultry are so difficult to break of this vice, that perhaps it would be wise for the dog-owner to pass a beloved pet to a professional dog-trainer for help. It is perhaps expedient to mention that certain breeds of dogs are more prone to certain types of stock-worrying than others. Whippets and other small sight hounds will often ignore sheep but be the very devil to break to cats, which are roughly the same size and shape as the natural quarry such dogs are bred and trained to hunt. Other breeds – I have already mentioned the unusually high incidence of sheep-worrying Irish setters and Dalmatians; collies of all types, bearded, border or rough, are invariably animated by the sight of a flock of sheep – and still more animated when they observe a single sheep feeding apart from the flock. Spitz breeds are particularly prone to sheep-worrying and while I know of a chow-chow that is one of the most stock-steady dogs I have ever seen, I have never encountered malemutes or Siberian huskies that I would consider allowing off the leash in sheep country.

The present trend to allow the British countryside to be used for recreational facilities means that far more dogs will be taken there by their owners. It is a dog-owner's duty to ensure that his pets are always under control and completely stock-steady.

10

Sit, Lie and Stay Training

It seems to be a British tradition that field sport magazines publish such ludicrous statements that the thinking members of the public are likely to roar with laughter when they read such nonsense. The most famous however was made in 1945 when two eminent fox-hunters stated that the fox actually enjoyed the chase as much as the hounds pursuing it. More recently another one slipped through the editorial gauntlet of a popular sporting magazine. The letter, concerned with the admirable practice of obedience-training lurchers stated, 'The lurcher fraternity is divided into two categories: those who hunt their dogs and those who train them to sit, lie and stay.' It would be difficult to imagine a more ludicrous, senseless comment – though indeed the dog fraternity might well be divided into two categories: those who train their dogs to sit, lie and stay, and those whose dogs are frequently a nuisance to all they encounter. A well-trained, obedient dog is indeed a pleasure to own – an untrained brute is something less than desirable. I like Roger Mugford's description of the role dogs play in man's life – 'they raise our self-esteem, make us laugh, introduce us to friendly people' – but a wild, badly trained animal certainly lowers our self-esteem, makes us cry, and alienates us from society generally. To reduce the training of a dog to sit, lie and stay, and all the other training that makes it a pleasure to own, to the level of simply teaching a dog tricks is absolutely absurd.

Why is it important to teach a dog to sit, lie or to stay? I ask you to visit a busy shopping precinct, and watch the interplay between the typical pet-owner and his dog. A lady laden with shopping has stopped, dog on leash, to talk to a friend. The dog, however, wishes to proceed and tugs repeatedly at the leash, almost toppling the woman and showering the pavement with sundry items of shopping. A gentleman is attempting to open the door of his car while his dog, excited at the prospect of the ride, is frantically tugging and scratching at the door as if to encourage the owner to speed up the process of allowing him access to the rear seat. A lady has opened the door of her hatchback and her dog, eager to be out, has leaped from the rear of the car and ploughed headlong into another shopper who is carrying goods to her car. It must be a nightmare to own such dogs, yet a few minutes a day spent in training these dogs to sit, lie and stay would have remedied the behaviour of such animals.

Training a puppy to sit is simplicity itself once the dog is lead-trained – lead-training is of course an essential prelude to most training programmes, particularly those a dog may not find quite as enjoyable as others. If a puppy is not lead-trained it can terminate a training exercise when and where it wishes simply by walking away from the handler, and while most training programmes can, with some thought, be made into a game or an enjoyable romp, few dogs actually enjoy sit, lie and stay training no matter how it is taught. So before teaching a puppy to sit (and then lie and stay) a puppy should be not only willing but happy to accept a leash and collar.

Basically there are two methods of teaching a puppy (or a grown dog) to sit, and all other 'sit' training methods are simply variations on a theme. Puppies seldom enjoy the practice of either method, one should add, but as with all training programmes the dog should be made to feel at ease when learning, and should never come to regard its training sessions as odious chores it would like to avoid.

Once the dog accepts the lead, sit-training should begin. With the puppy on the lead, close to the handler's side, the handler should press down on the puppy's rump uttering the word 'sit' as he does so. Both puppies and adult dogs are usually bewildered by the handler's actions when he starts to press their hind quarters to the ground and the majority of dogs will attempt to move away. However, the newcomer to dog-training will be astonished how quickly the dog comes to associate the action of dropping on its haunches to the sit position with the word 'sit', particularly if the dog has been rewarded with praise or food. There is a tendency for modern trainers not to reward dogs with titbits during a training session, and apparently it is decidedly *infra dig.* for a dog to seek a reward for every training exercise it attempts. This is clearly rubbish – the notion that when one day the dog is not rewarded for its success at a particular exercise it might become rebellious is so ludicrous that the would-be trainer should ignore this advice. It is, however, a fact that horses that are constantly given titbits for coming to hand do become somewhat difficult to manage when they are disappointed by the absence of titbits, but horses will never enjoy the reciprocal relationship with man that the dog has enjoyed for countless millenia. If a dog works well when given rewards of food, or works better to titbits than to praise, by all means use food as a reward.

An alternative method of teaching the sit position is to walk the dog on the leash and halt suddenly, yanking the dog's head slightly with the choke chain, while swinging the body to the left with one's right hand raised over the dog's head, and uttering the command 'sit' as one does so. This was once a popular method of teaching the 'sit' position and most post-war dog-training books – and there was a seemingly enormous market for such manuals immediately after World War II – suggested using it. My first really well-trained dog – a lurcher type with an extremely dubious pedigree – was subjected to this training technique for nearly a month, with somewhat poor results. Eventually I abandoned this method in favour of forcing down the dog's hind quarters while uttering the command 'sit'. In a matter of a day my lurcher puppy sat on command promptly, without needing additional signals or gestures. Since then I have avoided the hand-above-the dog's-head method of sit-training though I have seen many excellent, well-behaved dogs taught by this method. Training a dog, or any animal for that matter, requires a flexible approach and certain trainers are more adept at using particular methods than others, just as certainly as dogs respond to particular ways of teaching better than they do to other methods. The hand-above-the-head sit-training method is fine. I never became adept at using this technique.

Sit-training should not proceed too long so that it bores, upsets or intimidates the puppy. A few minutes of this sort of training each day is in fact much better than one lengthy, rather soul-destroying session that so upsets the puppy that it develops a look of despair when its owner takes out a leash to commence another training session. Once it becomes a chore further training that day is counter-productive. Puppies should always look forward to a training session: if it has not gone well or the relationship between dog and man is seen to sour, training should stop abruptly and the puppy encouraged to indulge in a game before being kennelled, leashed or brought home. No dog should dread the prospect of a training session and the trainer should never be regimented in his approach to training. Time spent thinking up ways to make a training session more enjoyable to a puppy is indeed time well spent. In fact during the time I spent in teacher-training the only wisdom I ever gleaned was a quotation from William James: 'The essential difference between play and work lies not in the nature of the activity itself but in the attitude of the doer towards it.' In short, if an exercise can be taught by making the training into a game almost all men + animals learn more quickly than they will if they regard the training session as an odious chore.

If the dog sits instantly when the command word 'sit' is uttered, it should be rewarded by praise or titbits – though the 'reward', should it be a display of affection from the owner, should never be so effusive as to cause the puppy to move from the sitting position. Each evening walk should include a few sit-training sessions to constantly reinforce the activity – for dogs, like human beings, tend to forget. Once again, the dog must never start to regard the evening stroll as a monotonous training session, and a romp or wild game should always be part of day-to-day exercise programmes for any breed of dog.

Teaching a dog to assume the 'down' position – early books concerned with dog-training insist on referring to this as the 'lie' position – is also relatively easy and is perhaps best attempted after the dog is conversant with sitting on command. Once again there are various methods of teaching a dog to assume the 'down' position.

The method advocated by most pet dog trainers is to leash the dog and command it to assume the sit position. Once the dog has assumed this position the trainer must exert firm but not forceful pressure on the puppy's shoulders and utter the command 'down' while doing so. This method of training will possibly create some slight confusion for the dog particularly if the 'sit' command precedes the 'down'. Many dogs put in the 'sit' position will assume the 'down' position before the trainer utters the command 'down' simply because the puppy is used to the customary progression, and possibly because many dogs are more comfortable when stationed in the 'down' position than they are in the 'sit'. Most professional trainers therefore avoid teaching 'down' from a 'sit' position and simply teach down by forcing the standing dog into the prone position without first sitting it. Professional dog-trainers, or those who train for competition, are only too aware of how easily a sitting dog will assume the 'down' position – partly because it may predict the command, and partly because most dogs naturally assume a 'down' position when at liberty. A dog left in a sitting position tends to gravitate to 'down' as soon as it becomes bored or slightly uncomfortable. Hence many trainers of competition dogs go to some pains to separate the 'sit' and 'down' training sessions with some other skill the dog is required to learn – retrieving or heel work, for example. Once a dog drops naturally without command from the 'sit' to the 'down' position the fault is a very difficult one to eradicate – though if the teaching of 'sit' or 'down' is simply a way of restraining the dog, its owner need not be overly worried if the dog that is required to sit assumes the 'down' position when it becomes slightly bored or uncomfortable.

Ensuring that the dog maintains the 'sit' or 'down' position while its handler is otherwise engaged is a natural progression in the training programme. At one time I confess I became the classic dog-training bore by encouraging friends to try and coax a dog from the 'sit' and 'down' positions in which I had left it. A psychologist friend witnessing my passion for this aspect of dog-training once remarked 'And God gave man dominion over animals' after he had witnessed my ostentatious and egocentric display of asking friends to break the 'dominion' I had over the dog. However, while I now regard my showmanship as a shade embarrassing, I can excuse my behaviour by stating that nothing gives a dog-trainer a greater lift than being able to train a dog to stay while the handler is out of sight. Furthermore it is perfectly natural for a person to wish to demonstrate or – to be more precise – to show off the skills he has taught his dog, or any other animal for that matter – which is why animal-training clubs stage events to demonstrate the skills they have taught their wards.

However, training a dog to stay at 'sit' or 'down' is far from pointless or ostentatious. To go back to our crowded shopping centre, with its badly-trained dogs bounding in or out of cars: it would be interesting to research just how many dogs leap out of cars into the path of other vehicles and not only come to grief by doing so but bring about horrendous accidents and loss of human life. Next to lead-training and teaching a dog to instantly come to hand, the sit/stay, down/stay aspect of training is the most important part of the education of the family dog.

In passing it may be expedient to mention that many police forces and military and security dog-training schools train the 'down' position in a rather unpleasant way. A switch is brought sharply across the dog's back, thereby encouraging it to drop instantly to avoid the pain it will experience if it remains standing. Konrad Most's *Dog Training* mentions that the majority of large, aggressive dogs given to police, security and military dog-training schools in Germany were taught the 'down' position in this way. Most defends the apparent cruelty of this method by stating that not only do these schools need to teach a dog quickly and thoroughly, but many of the dogs were given to these establishments because the dogs had begun to dominate the households in which they lived and had become extremely dangerous.

A police dog or an attack dog has to be trained to such a level of obedience that it will instantly release the person it is holding or attacking, and the most effective command to make a dog release its captive is 'down'. Hence attack dogs are taught to respond instantly to the command 'down' and the dog taught by means of a switch across the back will do just that.

At the risk of seeming a trifle effete, I must confess I have never used this method of teaching, and while I realise that it is efficacious, it would certainly not be a method I would recommend when training a puppy or an adult sight hound or sight-hound derivative. Although I have never achieved the instant responses I have witnessed in certain dog-training establishments in Germany and America, I still believe that a more gentle approach to training is more suitable for most dogs.

To teach a dog to stay in the 'down' position while its owner walks away or passes out of sight is quite an interesting and, for me at least, rewarding aspect of training. My own particular method of teaching it is to drop the dog to the 'sit' or 'down' position and back away from it, fixing it with my eyes and uttering 'down' or 'sit' if the dog attempts to follow me. Eye contact with an animal is an important aspect of control as anyone who has observed the behaviour of a group of adult dogs will have realised, and I make full use of it while teaching this exercise. I proceed quite gradually with 'stay' training, and try to minimise the panic a young dog is bound to experience when its owner appears to be abandoning it. Nervous dogs or puppies which have very strong bonds with their owners are often quite distressed when they see their handler backing away from them, but fixing the dog with one's eyes and repeating 'down' or 'sit' if it moves towards you will usually succeed in fixing all but the most nervous of dogs.

I repeat the process every day, and each time move further from the dog, still fixing it with my eyes as I do so. I make a point of returning to the dog and rewarding it with either effusive praise or titbits if it remains in the 'sit' or 'down' position for the length of time I require it to do so. No matter how tired I am and no matter how irksome the walk back to the dog may be, I never call the dog to me and reward it. Dogs are probably far more logical in their thinking than men: to call a dog to the handler and then reward it is to reward the action of coming to hand rather than the action of sitting or staying at the 'down' position for a certain length of time. When I return to the dog I make a point of praising the dog particularly effusively, for dogs dislike being made to stay behind when a handler moves off and I believe that when a dog completes what it considers to be an uncongenial task, the reward should be correspondingly great.

It is relatively easy to keep a dog at the 'stay' position while one has eye contact with it but once one loses eye contact the chances are that it will attempt to rise and follow the handler. I usually turn my back and walk away from the dog – thereby losing eye contact – only after I am able to back away (still fixing the dog with my eyes) from the dog for some twenty yards without the dog rising from the position in which I have left it.

When the time has come to turn and walk away from the dog I expect the dog to attempt to rise and follow me – in fact I would be surprised if it did not break its position so I pre-empt this by uttering 'down' or 'sit' as I move away from the animal. I once watched a lady who later became quite a celebrity in competitive dog-training circles perform this aspect of training, and noticed that despite the fact that the lady's back was turned to the dog, she knew exactly what was happening behind her and uttered 'stay' or 'down' or 'sit' at exactly the right moment to prevent the dog from rising to its feet to follow her. At first I thought the handler had an uncanny understanding of exactly when the dog was about to break – and the collie she was training was so attached to the handler that it was obviously upset when she lost eye contact with the dog – that I also considered the possibility that the dog shared a curious telepathic link with its owner. Perhaps the pair were so in tune with each other that they were able to predict each others movements – and I honestly believe I developed such a link with a terrier I once trained. On closer examination, however, I realised that the handler held a tiny fragment of mirror in her hand and by observing the reflection she knew exactly what the dog behind her was about to do. Any such props should always be utilised, regardless of how bizarre or Heath Robinson they may appear to those who have never trained a dog.

Once the dog has become used to the handler losing eye contact and walking away while it remains in the 'down' or sitting position, the training programme can progress one stage further, with the animal staying in the 'sit' or 'down' position while the handler is out of sight. This is best taught in a place where the handler, after uttering 'stay' or 'down' can pop behind a wall or tree, out of sight of the dog, but still able to immediately reappear and reprimand it if it rises and attempts to follow – and it most certainly will during the first few training sessions, for most dogs become extremely unhappy when their owners suddenly disappear from view. The majority of dogs faced with this situation for the very first time either rise and follow the handler or edge forward towards the point where he has disappeared.

It will almost certainly take many lessons to ensure that a dog will always stay put when its owner disappears from view, and I would advise the handler to perform this aspect of training as privately as possible. Not only is it likely that children and adults alike will notice a dog sitting or lying by itself and either speak to it or, worse still, attempt to stroke or pet it – and these actions are almost certain to ensure the dog 'breaks' position and attempts to seek out a handler – but furthermore the act of training a dog in a public place is almost certain to attract the notice of people who will be perturbed by the highly irregular behaviour of the dog-trainer – for people who have never trained a dog usually find the antics of the trainer and his dog hard to understand.

It is in fact often difficult for the dog-trainer to maintain any sense of dignity if he or she attempts to train a dog in a public place. Indeed I would advise anyone who believes that a sense of propriety, decorum and dignity should be maintained at all times to abandon any attempt to train a dog – or better still not to purchase a dog in the first place. The general public regard most dog-handlers as eccentric or even stark staring mad, and the apparently weird and irrational behaviour manifested by anyone attempting to train a dog often confirms this belief. When I lived in a crowded area of Rotherham I spent many hours training a German shepherd dog puppy, and I performed my training sessions during the early hours of the morning so that they would pass unnoticed by the general public. Thus as soon as dawn broke I would start training my puppy in an area near a large cemetery. The few early-morning spectators travelling to and from the local steel works did not bat an eyelid at the retrieving, walking to heel and jumping training sessions, but the training of a dog to stay in the 'sit' or 'lie' position while I passed out of sight of the dog, caused a great deal more interest, I'm afraid.

It was my practice to drop the dog to a 'sit' or 'down' position and then walk round the corner of a wall, press myself tight against the wall and wait to see if the dog rose and attempted to follow me. As I lived in a heavily populated area I performed this aspect of the training programme when there were few people around lest I should be regarded as a suitable case for treatment.

One morning, after I had dropped the dog to the 'down' position and was hiding behind the corner of a house, I observed the curtains of the house opposite move slightly, but decided not to concern myself with the fact someone was watching. However, an hour later, after I had engaged the dog in a wild romp, I resumed the staying-in-'down'-position training only to find that when I walked away and pressed myself against the wall, two police officers seated in a panda car were watching me. I must have seemed a complete lunatic – and frankly I expected to be taken into the local police station for questioning or find myself the subject of a psychiatric report. Fortunately the majority of police officers are extremely perspicacious, and the driver of the panda car simply stepped out of the car and asked, 'Will he stay at "down" if someone tries to call him?'. He told me he had applied to train as a dog-handler, so he obviously understood why I was behaving in a curious manner.

However the owner of a pet dog might well question the usefulness of such training to a dog-owner who doesn't want an animal to compete in the popular obedience tests that are run by dog-training groups. In fact, teaching a dog to stay put is far from being a totally useless exercise, and it should not be relegated to the level of teaching a dog 'tricks'. There are many occasions when a handler is out with the dog and needs to go to places where a dog would not be exactly welcome. Two such occasions occurred recently, and both accentuated just how important it is to own a dog that will stay put when it is required to do so.

A few days ago a white German shepherd male called Walden was at exercise in a lonely country lane near our cottage, and because there was no danger of traffic or any likelihood of causing upset to people (Walden is a large, wolf-like dog who could easily frighten anyone who came on him suddenly) he was allowed to run on ahead. A bleat indicated that a sheep pastured in the fields adjacent to the road was in distress and on approaching the fence I saw a ewe with its head jammed in the sheep wire. As Walden approached, the sheep became terrified and began to struggle so furiously that it appeared to be garrotting itself, so Walden was left at 'down' some twenty yards away from the sheep, while I extricated it from the tangle.

Another instance occurred in Wick some five years ago. A young child slipped and fell in the car park near the main shopping centre apparently damaging her leg. A young man with a rottweiler male on a leash, rushed over to help the child taking the dog with him. At that time rottweilers were regarded as demon dogs – a role later to be assumed by pit bull terriers – and shots of huge aggressive rottweilers were always being shown on television news programmes. The child became hysterical as the dog came towards her, and the rottweiler, I would guess it to have been a puppy of a year or so, misinterpreted her screams and attempted to play with her. An unpleasant situation promptly escalated to one of extreme danger. Had the young man trained the dog to stay put at the 'down' or 'sit' position he could have helped the child. As it was her frantic screams attracted a crowd who, seeing the large and powerful rottweiler, promptly came to the conclusion the dog had attacked the child. It is interesting to note that two women went to the aid of the child but several bulky males refrained from interfering!

If you walk in the centre of a busy town or city you will see the numerous dog-owners being towed along the pavements by unruly dogs. At pedestrian crossings the dog takes over and pulls its handler across the road whether or not the road light indicates danger or the figure of a pedestrian beckons those on foot to cross. It is decidedly dangerous to own such an untrained animal. If the handler had only spent a few minutes a day training the dog to sit at the curbside until it was safe to cross, the dangers attendant on owning a large, powerful dog in a crowded town could have been reduced. Once, while travelling through Paris in a taxi driven by what seemed to be a homicidal lunatic, I observed a young woman being towed into the fast-moving traffic by two black German shepherd dogs. Both the woman and her dogs were struck by oncoming cars, but my driver seemed unmoved by the accident. It is indeed '*un homme sans merci*' who drives a cab in Paris, I thought.

Professional dog-handlers who train guard and attack dogs – and a recent *exposé* has indicated just how many trainers deliberately train dogs to attack intruders despite the British laws regarding the use of guard dogs – frequently use the command 'down – stay' to restrain a dog that is attacking a person. This has an imperative note about it and, coupled with the way many dogs are taught to 'drop' to command, has the effect of making the dog release its hold on its foe.

To claim that a dog that has been taught to sit, lie or stay is simply a dog that has been taught rather useless and pointless tricks is ridiculous. This programme is in fact one of the most important aspects of training for any breed of dog from the Yorkshire terrier to the Irish wolfhound.

11

Jumping

I have, I hope, persuaded the pragmatic reader that it is essential to teach a family pet dog to sit, lie and stay, even if it is not destined to compete in trails and competitions. It is equally important to teach it to jump, as the following example – involving once again the average dog-owner at large with his totally untrained pet – should make plain. The interaction of the two species will make the most learned cynologist question whether *homo sapiens* have ever enjoyed a symbiotic relationship with *canis familiaris*!

A woman, large dog on leash, is waiting for her husband to return to their hatchback car after a shopping expedition, so that he, groaning, sweating and cursing all shopping trips, can lift the dog into the back of the car. This couple are doomed to a life of urban weekends and holidays if they decide to take the dog with them wherever they go. The countryside, with its fast-disappearing right of ways, is littered with stiles and low fences over which the husband must lift his huge dog, so that a country ramble takes on the nature of a Charles Atlas limbering-up session. The couple suffer the agonies of Sisyphus as the dog is lifted and pushed over stiles and stone walls and return from what should have been an invigorating walk in the country as exhausted as a Marine recruit undergoing officer selection exercises. Should the reader believe my stories of the horrors of keeping an untrained dog are exaggerated, may I suggest that he interviews a person who has kept a large, untrained dog and asks if he would consider keeping a dog of any breed again. Dogs should be kept to give the owner pleasure, entertainment and a fuller, more interesting life, yet a great many of them contribute only grief, misery, expense and inconvenience and the fault, dear Brutus, is with ourselves. Yet in fact teaching a dog to jump is not only easy, but enjoyable for both the trainer and the dog.

So easy is it to train a dog to jump that whenever I breed a litter of lurcher puppies they are usually taught to jump before I allow them to leave the premises. This must seem a somewhat curious sales gimmick to the uninitiated reader, but the fact is that lurchers, by the very nature of their work, need to be able to jump, yet on account of the type of people who own them, they are some of the worst trained dogs imaginable. In 1981 I was asked to look at a lurcher, whose owner claimed it to be one of the best hare-catching dogs in Britain. Now the hare is a mighty adversary for any dog, and it invariably evades capture by using all sorts of objects and obstacles to throw off the dog that is pursuing it. Fences are used to good advantage by a hare, and a dog that cannot jump is unlikely to catch one. The particular dog, a powerfully built longdog rather than a lurcher, sprung its hare, and to my amazement its owner ran off after it. I was amazed – that is, until I observed the hare pass through a fence with the dog hot on its heels. The longdog simply refused to try to jump the fence and raced up and down the sheep wire until its owner arrived and flung it over the fence, thereby allowing the chase to continue. Three fences were negotiated in this manner and needless to say the hare escaped capture easily. Yet lurchers are the most easily taught 'jumpers', and there are accounts of dogs of this type scaling huge obstacles with great ease.

Teaching lurcher puppies to jump is extremely simple. I place a board some six inches high across the kennel doorway and call them to feed. It is a very strange whelp which does not scramble over the obstacle with ease, and the physical skill of jumping is acquired in moments. Later I increase the height of the board to a foot, and once again call the puppies to feed; and I have yet to see an eight-week-old lurcher puppy which found it difficult to scramble over an obstacle of this height. Long before my whelps are ready to leave me they will hop, scramble or jump over a board some two-feet-six in height.

I witnessed the most amazing display of puppies jumping great obstacles in 1986. A lurcher-breeder, Josie Woodhouse, had held back a litter until they were twelve weeks old before parting with them, and by a simple progression process had taught them the skill of jumping. The whelps were enclosed in a paddock by six-feet-high chain-link fencing, and at mealtimes Mrs Woodhouse simply called them and they scrambled over the wire fence to their feeding bowls. Personally, I feel that this may be asking a shade too much of puppies of this age, for while the whelps easily scaled the wires, they landed heavily on the concrete slab path outside the enclosure: I believe that when an animal lands heavily on its paws it can damage the cartilage that buffers the contact point of the leg.

It is in fact possible to teach any dog to jump, though clearly some dogs are more athletic than others. Sight hounds and sight-hound derivatives are easily taught to jump quite sizeable objects, and to spring over ditches and brooks with great ease. German shepherd dogs, collies and retrievers are also amongst the winners at competitive jumping displays. Yet one of the most appealing sights at obedience and agility tests is that of tiny toy breeds such as poodles and Pomeranians scaling and scrambling over boards and obstacles with alacrity and great enthusiasm. Tiny Schnauzers are, in fact, extremely popular at competitions that involve jumping and scrambling techniques.

There are basically two distinct methods of training the family dog to jump and both are equally efficacious in teaching it to scale walls, stiles, or leap into the backs of cars.

Calling-on training has already been described – and

consists of simply placing a series of boards across the front of a dog's kennel or across a passageway and enticing the dog to scale the obstruction to come to its owner. Dogs should enjoy the process of being trained to jump and should never be allowed to train on rickety equipment which is likely to rock or fall when the dog is scaling it. If a dog is injured during jumping training it is often difficult to get it to jump again. A dog that is injured or hurt after it has been trained and enjoys the action of jumping will often forget the injuries it sustains, but a youngster injured while scaling an unsafe hurdle may well refuse to jump again for some time.

The calling-on method of training a dog to jump should always start by using a board or a solid object through which the dog cannot see, to block the passageway between the dog and the handler. If the passageway is blocked by wire fencing, through which the dog can see, it will usually try to push its way through the spaces in the netting rather than jump the obstacle. Many adult dogs will in fact jump wooden structures through which they cannot see but refrain from jumping sheep netting – and the sight of a dog running up and down a low fence seeking a spot through which it can creep is an extremely common one. Dogs taught the calling-on method of jumping should be kept away from wire fences until they are completely competent at leaping solid hurdles.

The other method of teaching a dog to jump is often referred to as running-up training. It cannot be taught until the dog is not only lead-broken, but is completely at ease when made to wear a collar or choke chain and leash. The running-up method should also start by a board some six inches high being placed across a passageway. The trainer, with the dog on a leash, steps over the board, jerking the lead slightly as he does so and uttering the word 'up' or 'over' as the puppy steps or scrabbles over the board. If the puppy can be made to experience excitement or enjoyment as it attempts this, so much the better – in fact any exercise that is taught as a game is usually more successful than the same exercise taught as a chore. I usually engage the puppy in some sort of exciting game before jumping it over the board. Most breeds of dog can easily step over a six-inch board, and a few sessions each day is usually enough to encourage the whelp to hop or step over it. The exercise should finish with a romp.

The puppy should associate running-up training with great pleasure.

On the day following the puppy's introduction to jumping-training, the board can be raised by an inch or so. The trainer must use his or her common sense regarding the amount the 'jumping frame' is to be made higher – an athletic adult dog will obviously be able to progress much faster than a puppy from a small toy breed, but no dog of any age or breed should be over-matched by raising the jump too high or too quickly, and above all the exercise must be taught as an exciting game. Watch the puppy – its mannerisms or facial expressions will reveal much of its mood: if the puppy looks unwilling to participate in the game, avoid training for that day or engage it in some activity the animal finds enjoyable.

There will of course come a time when the height of the jump is raised to such a level that the owner is unable to step over it. Then the trainer should run the leashed dog to the hurdle and step to the right or left as the dog jumps the obstacle, jerking the leash and uttering the word 'up' or 'over' as the dog arrives at the hurdle.

Handlers who wish to compete in the jumping competitions that were once so popular at country shows (and are becoming popular once again, so it appears) should teach a dog to jump by the running-up method rather than the calling-on technique.

The collie lurcher, Blue, owned by Corporal Alan Hooten, was an extremely successful competition dog and was seldom bettered in competitive jumping events in the 1980s. Blue's great party piece was to jump the goalposts on the soccer pitches around Doncaster, and its owner won considerable sums of money when the dog performed this spectacular jump. Blue was one of the few top competition jumpers that was taught by the calling-on method, one should add.

Sooner or later a dog will topple a hurdle or cause some obstacle to fall while it is jumping or scaling, and sustain either fright or injury as a result. If the dog is merely frightened, and not hurt, then a profuse show of affection from its handler will usually counteract the fright it has received. If the dog is injured, however, or winded by its fall – and I have seen many dogs so winded as to be unable to rise – it is best to allow the dog to recover before petting or fussing over it. At some of the show-jumping events dogs have scaled such incredible heights that the jump to the ground is injurious. These days straw bales are strategically placed on the far side of the jumps so that the dog has a fairly soft landing, but during competitions of the early 1980s few show organisers seemed aware of the damage to a dog's paws that was often sustained when a dog scrambled nine feet and was required to leap back on to hard compacted ground.

During this era one of my lurchers competed with considerable success though finally I withdrew my dog from competition as persistent landing on hard soil was causing damage to the cartilage in his wrists.

It is fair to say that I never trained a dog more enthusiastic about jumping than was Burke, my competition dog. He jumped for the fun of it as a young puppy, despite the fact that he sustained a wrist injury when he was fourteen weeks of age. He scaled tennis court fences with ease after developing a technique of striking the spot where the mesh was likely to belly and then scrambling up the mesh from his point of impact. As time went on I noticed that he became terribly excited when asked to jump an object and never once refused to attempt a leap. So I entered him at the competitive events at country fairs. It is said that some racehorses refuse to allow another horse to get ahead of them – and, at the risk of appearing anthropomorphic, I believe Burke enjoyed hard competition. When his most serious competition was present at an event he jumped better than ever, and in four years I never once lost a jumping event with him. After his first season his desire to jump became almost obsessive. As soon as I arrived at the showground and he noticed a jumping frame being constructed, he became wild with delight and had to be restrained. It became common practice for me to stay at the far side of the showground while the hurdles and frames were being constructed, for when he was allowed to watch them being built he became almost exhausted with excitement. I enjoyed owning him and perhaps gloried in the fact that Burke was virtually impossible to beat at the activity he loved best, but I cannot but think he was slightly deranged. A good tale needs a good ending, so I shall finish my story of Burke. I retired him when he was six years of age, for he became increasingly lame as the competition season progressed. At the end of his seventh year while chasing a hare, he jumped a hedge and fell heavily on some antique, rusting farm equipment, breaking his neck and dying instantly. I feel that the nature of his demise was the way he would have wished it to be – and if my opinion seems unscientific and totally anthropomorphic I make no apology for my beliefs. His qualities were not inherited by his daughter Fathom. She was a serious, almost mirthless puppy who jumped well until, at the age of two, she damaged her feet and shattered her shoulder blades. I ceased jumping her forthwith, and another jumper of the like of Burke has yet to appear in the strain. In many ways it is perhaps for the best – a mania for jumping is not necessarily healthy, or always convenient.

I always teach dogs what is commonly, though inaccurately, known as long-jumping. Most dogs take to this activity with greater willingness than they do scaling or leaping over obstacles and frames. Once again it is perhaps a good idea to explain why it is essential to teach a dog to bound across a space. The typical dog-owner lives in urban surroundings and usually travels to the countryside by car or public transport to exercise himself and his pet. The ditches surrounding or separating fields are not merely ornamental features but are constructed to allow water or animal waste to drain away from fields or buildings. It is seldom good sense to allow a dog to paddle through such ditches and become covered with mud, filth or toxic chemicals. In the early 1960s three dogs apparently died after paddling through a ditch that drained a field on which toxic chemicals had been used. These deaths alerted the public to the dangers afoot in the countryside and certainly gave Rachel Carson much publicity for her masterly book *Silent Spring* but did little for either the dogs or their owners.

Teaching an average dog to jump across spaces is simplicity itself. Once the dog has been taught to hop over a small hurdle, two hurdles should be placed parallel to one another, the dog is then led up to the hurdles, the lead is jerked and the command 'over' or 'up over' uttered. As the training programme progresses the hurdles should be moved further and further apart and the dog required to leap across the space. A third hurdle placed in the middle will usually be efficacious in preventing the dog from hopping one hurdle and then the other. Most dogs – even tiny toy dogs – are capable of springing across a four-feet gap, and once a dog has learned this technique it is capable of leaping across the average ditch after its handler.

A word now about that scourge of the countryside, barbed wire – the most devilish invention devised by man, though apparently patented by a woman. This horrendous stock deterrent is capable of inflicting awful wounds on any dog that attempts a jump and misses its footing in the take-off, or touches a line or barb in mid-flight. More dogs are injured by lines of wire than the average dog owner realises, and it is wise to take precautions to reduce the risk of injury when the handler exercises his dog in the countryside – for despite the fact that the British have a reputation for being over-sensitive about the welfare of animals, no race in the world makes more use of barbed wire than the British landowner and stock-keeper.

Some dogs seem to be inherently suspicious of barbed wire. At the moment the most athletic dog I have in my kennels is a saluki/greyhound longdog, a hybrid that is not exactly famed for its intelligence but is wonderfully athletic. My longdog apparently inherited some innate skill at negotiating barbed-wire fences. She seems to sense whether the fence she is about to jump is topped with a strand of wire, and then clears the fence with two feet to spare. To date she has never been injured by the tines of wire that have gashed and torn so many of my other dogs.

Not all dogs are as lucky, and most dogs need some help negotiating fences topped with barbed wire. I usually try to cover the patch of wire a dog is about to jump by placing my arm (shielded by my jacket sleeve, I should add) so that its hind legs touch my arm rather than the tines of the wire. To date I have not been injured by shielding the dog from the wire in this manner, though it is obvious that this technique has its dangers. A jacket or sack placed across the fence at the point the dog is required to jump will invariably prevent the dog damaging itself and be far less dangerous to the handler than allowing one's arm to act as a buffer.

To own a dog that has never been taught to jump is a nuisance, and the technique of jumping is so easily learned that all dogs can be taught. Most dogs enjoy the action of jumping and it would be a strange handler indeed that did not experience pleasure from training the dog.

12

Dogs and Water

It is an excellent policy to encourage a dog to paddle or swim in streams and shallow rivers, particularly if its owner has a penchant for rambling or lives in the country. In fact there are few more absurd sights than a handler crossing a shallow stream, while the dog runs up and down the bank refusing to cross. The sight of the handler wading waist-deep in the stream carrying a heavy dog is even more ridiculous – particularly as the majority of dogs enjoy paddling or swimming in streams if, that is, they are brought into contact with water gradually, and the handler uses good old-fashioned common sense in the way he introduces his dog to fairly large expanses of water.

Some breeds are less enthusiastic about entering water than others. Certain breeds have in fact been deliberately bred to retrieve water-fowl that have been shot dead or wounded and fallen into deep water. Such breeds have – or at least should have – a great affinity with water. Sadly, over the last few years, field trial reports indicate that many of these dogs are now rather water-shy and can only with difficulty be persuaded to fetch game from water.

Curiously, pet-owners are frequently amazed when they observe poodles deliberately swimming out into deep and fast-flowing water. In point of fact they too were bred to retrieve game from water. When the Celts migrated from Central Europe to France, Spain, Britain and Italy, Roman historians remarked on the curious water dogs which accompanied the migrating tribes. In all probability these dogs were the ancestors of the poodle, and several other breeds of dog. It would be difficult to find a more versatile dog than the poodle, whether standard, miniature or toy.

Labradors, and the somewhat rarer Newfoundlands – at one time one of the most popular breeds in Britain – are probably descended from a common stock. According to Carson Ritchie, both breeds may have descended from Eskimo dogs and from some breed similar in type and pedigree to the Pyrenean mountain dog. It is generally believed that both the Labrador and the Newfoundland were descended from dogs carried aboard the dories of the Basque fishermen who worked the deeps off Newfoundland for cod. Dogs of this type were used to carry messages between ships, or to kill giant cod that thrashed and snapped around the cramped decks of the dories. Landseer painted one such dog, a pied Newfoundland of the type that R. M. Ballantyne made the hero of his book *The Dog Crusoe*, calling his portrait 'A distinguished member of the Royal Humane Society' (a society devoted to saving those in danger of drowning). Labrador retrievers are in fact believed to be a smaller type of Newfoundland, that became popular with rough-shooters and wildfowlers. Both breeds show a natural propensity to enter water, and need little encouragement to venture out into deep and turbulent rivers. One such dog – quite likely of the base stock that spawned both Newfoundlands and Labradors – served with a corps of life-saving dogs on the banks of the Seine prior to the Franco-Prussian War. So enthusiastic was it that it had to be restrained from trying to rescue ordinary swimmers who were not in any difficulty!

For some reason sight hounds – greyhounds, whippets, deerhounds wolfhounds, borzois, salukis etc. – have a reputation for being reluctant or unwilling to enter deep water. Many breed books (though probably not those written by true enthusiasts who should subject their work to greater scrutiny before publishing) attribute this reluctance to the fact that sight hounds originated in the arid regions of the Middle East where they would have been unlikely to encounter large expanses of water. Clearly such a theory does not stand up to close scrutiny: it presupposes that the breed did indeed originate in the Middle East (and there is no evidence to support this theory) and that all sight hounds are descended from a common stock – for which again there is absolutely no evidence. Whatever the reasons, pure-bred sight hounds are usually reluctant to enter water – in 1990 *Shooting News* published a letter concerning the reluctance of most lurchers to do so.

Spitz-type breeds, ostiaks, malemutes, samoyeds, Siberian huskies and chow-chows also have a reputation for being shy of entering water, and once again many breed books offer explanations. One theory (and this stand up to fairly close scrutiny) is that they originated in the Arctic regions, where conditions would have made a wet dog an extremely dead dog – for water freezes extremely rapidly during an Arctic winter. So water-shy are some of these dogs that travellers record that sled dogs are reluctant to pass over ice that is flawed and likely to give way under the weight of the sled. In 1925 a freak snowstorm swept Alaska and grounded the airforce. Temperatures fell to -60 degrees below zero, and the winds became gale-force. Visibility was reduced to near zero and life from Fairbanks to Nome and Pelee slowed to a standstill. Diphtheria, a lethal disease in the days prior to World War II, broke out in the Eskimo villages north of Nome, and serum needed to be transported there from Anchorage to inoculate the inhabitants of the Inuit villages, who had no immunity to diphtheria. A group of sled-dog enthusiasts decided to transport the serum – the phials of which were wrapped in rabbit fur to protect them from the freezing temperatures – the 655 miles from Anchorage to Nome. On the last leg of the journey Kasson, a veteran sled-dog enthusiast, harnessed an equally antique sled dog, Balto, to the lead position and set off to cross Norton Sound. Balto refused to face the ice despite the urgings of Kasson, and seconds later the ice gave way with a thunderous roar. It is believed that the Siberian husky's reluctance to face water may have prompted the dog to refuse to cross the unsafe ice. It is equally likely that the groans and creaks of the shifting ice plates frightened the dog, in the same way that the groaning and creaking of wooden pit-props alerts a pit pony to the movement of the 'roof' in a coal mine. Still, it's a good tale and I make no apologies for including it in a book concerned with dog-training.

Yet even spitz breeds and sight hounds can be encouraged to walk through brooks or streams and even swim rivers and bays should the handler require them to do so – provided they are gradually encouraged into the water, which should become progressively deeper and more faster flowing each day of the training session. If the dog is suddenly introduced to cold, deep water and is frightened by its first encounter, it is often difficult to train it to swim past the point where its feet do not touch the bottom of the pond or river. Dog-trainers of yesteryear advocated a whelp should be taken to a deep river, thrown in and required to swim to the bank. This method supposedly taught the dog to swim. This, of course, is absolute lunacy for all dogs have the technique of swimming after a fashions, but the art is to train the dog to willingly take to water whenever the handler requires it to do so. This short, sharp shock treatment is decidedly damaging to the confidence of the dog and is extremely likely to make even a Labrador, or another breed with a fondness for water, extremely shy of entering deep water.

When I first came to Caithness, my German shepherd, bitch Polly was used to work in a creel boat. For those not *au fait* with maritime terminology, a creel boat is a small craft – my own was sixteen feet long – that is used to set and retrieve crab traps in rocky inlets around the coast. Each crab trap, or creel, is marked by a buoy attached to the creel by some sixty feet of rope. The creels are often set in very shallow spots in rocky reefs into which it is exceedingly difficult to sail a boat. Hence Polly was trained to jump from the boat, swim to the buoy, seize the rope attaching it to the creel and swim back to the boat, bringing it with her. The local fishermen remarked at her intelligence and prowess and she must have appeared the ideal dog for working in water. Yet it was the devil's own job to entice her into the sea for she had been terrified by an early mishap involving deep water.

Shortly after Polly was immunised against the four major canine ills (distemper, hardpad, hepatitis and leptospiral jaundice) she was taken on her first lead-training session near the canal at Whittington. She disliked the lead intensely, so to make the training less odious for the twelve-week-old puppy I engaged her in a wild romp as soon as the lead-training became tiresome to her. Perhaps my choice of location for the game was unwise, for the surface of the canal was covered in a thin layer of algae which Polly mistook for solid ground. After her first lead-training session she ran to the bank and attempted to run across the surface of the water. She disappeared from view for a second or so and surfaced with a panic-stricken expression on her face. Polly was obviously terrified by the experience and next day she trembled with fear when I attempted to put her on the leash.

The romp was supposed to make Polly less unhappy about being lead-trained. As it was it had the reverse effect. She associated lead-training with the stark terror of her submersion in the canal and became terrified when my lead-training session took her in its direction. Matters became so bad that I finally took to putting a leash on her just before she was fed so that she associated the act of being leashed up with the pleasure she experienced when feeding. Even so, at first she refused to feed when she felt the pressure of the leash and choke chain around her neck.

Ironically, she associated her fearsome ordeal on the canal with lead-training, not with the presence of water and shortly after she became steady with the leash again – at first matters were so bad that she fouled herself when I produced the leash – I walked her through some woods near my cottage and she plodded through a shallow stream with only slight trepidation. However for a full year after the submersion she was fearful of a walk along the canal bank.

My customary practice is to train dogs to enter water by allowing them to follow me as I wade into a shallow stream. There are few dogs that will not follow their owners to the point where the dog starts to tread water. It often takes a lot more persuasion to make a dog follow when the water becomes so deep that the dog has to tread water and start to swim. Yet swimming is instinctive to all wild canids even to desert foxes such as the fennec, a species that seldom encounters water, so dogs need never be taught to swim (I've never understood the expression 'teaching a dog to swim' anyway). However, they do need to be given confidence or motivation to walk into progressively deeper water and finally start the process of swimming.

If a puppy is a persistent retriever or if it has a particularly beloved toy it likes to retrieve, then a dummy or the toy can be dropped into the shallows, and the puppy will usually paddle in to fetch it. Once it is accustomed to getting its feet wet, the object can be cast into slightly deeper water and the puppy encouraged to walk out to fetch it. When the object is cast into water that is so deep that the puppy needs to tread water or swim to recover it, I usually generate a great deal of excitement in the whelp before throwing the dummy or toy. My usual technique is to show the whelp the object to be thrown, snatch it away as the puppy reaches for it and I then tease the whelp to the point where it becomes excited and frantic to seize the dummy or toy. Only then is the toy or dummy cast into deeper water into which the whelp has to swim to recover the object. If the puppy is reluctant to tread water, but runs around the shallows eager to retrieve the object, although reluctant to swim to recover it, I fetch the dummy or toy and engage the whelp in a game of retrieving before throwing the object into deeper water again. The secret of persuading any dog to take to water is to make haste slowly, never to rush the whelp, never to frighten the animal and never to overtax its newly discovered skill of swimming by casting the dummy too far from *terra firma*.

If at any time during the training a puppy becomes frightened or exhausted and fearful of drowning, or experiences pain that it associates with the action of swimming, it might be advisable to start training the puppy in the shallows again or – and I have found this far more efficacious – to quit water-training sessions for a full week or so, but visit the river, pond or seashore where the puppy is to be trained and engaging the puppy in an exciting game near the spot where it has experienced pain, discomfort or fear. Only when the puppy shows pleasure at the prospect of visiting the area near which water-training was given, should it be encouraged back into deep water. Time is often a great healer where dogs are concerned particularly if the owner exercises commonsense when reintroducing the whelp to a situation that has caused the puppy anxiety.

The majority of dogs enjoy swimming once they have acquired confidence enough to tread water and slip into the action of swimming. Lest the reader should think I have left a tale half told – a heinous fault no professional writer should ever commit – it might be expedient to explain how Polly was taught to swim into the sea near the rocks of Mey, seize a length of creel line and return creel line and float to the boat. The action while it looked spectacular and extremely difficult to teach was in fact simplicity itself for Polly to learn and required only a degree of common sense on the part of the trainer.

Polly was taught to retrieve a length of line of the type used to attach a creel to the buoy. When she became dexterous at fetching the line, a light float (I used a half gallon plastic milk carton) was attached to the line and Polly sent to retrieve both line and float. If I had used a heavier float, that would have caused some discomfort or, worse still, hurt her while she was retrieving it, in which case Polly would have experienced a negative sensation when sent to retrieve the float and line, hence the use of the Heath Robinson milk carton device during the initial training sessions.

When Polly was proficient at fetching the line and somewhat heavier float (by now I was using a lightweight plastic buoy) and obviously experienced pleasure from fetching the contraption the entire length of the quay, then the line and buoy were dropped into the shallows near the harbour slipway and she was encouraged to paddle in to fetch it. Later, the line and buoy were dropped into the deeper water beyond the slip and Polly encouraged to swim out and retrieve the contraption, but once again I adopted the *festina lente* dictum and proceeded slowly in the training programme, halting and changing tack when Polly ceased to enjoy herself.

Our first spell of actually retrieving a line that was attached to both creel and buoy was practised in the sheltered areas near the harbour where strong currents and high waves would not frighten or hurt Polly, but within a month she was working at fetching creel ropes along the most dangerous stretch of shore line in Britain. To persuade her to go over the side of the boat to fetch the creel I required (and not someone else's creel ropes, for nothing alienates a man living in a crabbing community more than the act of lifting someone's creels) I took along a handful of small pebbles. I would utter 'fetch' and then throw a pebble near to the creel line. Polly would then leap overboard and seize the line nearest to where she saw the splash and return that rope to the boat. Her work probably saved many hours of boat repair. I retired her early in 1988, as she developed quite bad arthritis, and oddly enough I smashed the shaft of my outboard motor the month after I ceased using her. She died quietly in 1990, an old, fat lady for whom life had been fun, but a month before her demise, during a lull in her arthritis, I took her to the beach near the harbour from which she once worked. A storm had blown up the week previous and the shoreline was littered with debris. I saw her rush along the beach and return to me with a line in her mouth – the line attached to a shattered plastic buoy and a very buckled creel.

I believe Polly would have prefered to work until the day of her death and I never once regretted the lengthy periods I spent training her.

13

Retrieving

It could be argued that if the pet owner is not a shooting man who can use the animal as a gun dog, teaching the family pet to retrieve serves no useful purpose whatsoever. If one wishes to be entirely pragmatic about the ownership of a dog then I suppose such a statement is true, but retrieving-training is such good fun for both the dog and the trainer that it is well worthwhile training a dog to fetch any object one wishes to be brought to hand. Owning a dog is or rather should be fun and the more one puts into any venture the more one expects to get out of that venture. I confess I have had a great deal of fun out of teaching dogs to retrieve and have yet to own a dog that did not enjoy being taught to fetch certain objects.

Some breeds of dog show a natural propensity to retrieve, while others are less enthusiastic. Breeds such as Labradors, curly-coated, flat-coated and golden retrievers are, by the very nature of the work for which they were bred, relatively easy dogs to teach – though many golden retrievers have a reputation for being reluctant or intermittent retrievers until they start to mature. Most types of spaniel show a natural inclination to fetch objects to hand, but collies, German shepherd dogs and various terriers are often equally enthusiastic. Sight hounds are often reluctant retrievers or become bored with retrieving all too quickly and they have to be taught in a rather special manner. It is interesting to note that many competent professional dog-trainers are shy of taking on sight hounds for obedience training simply because they usually have a relatively low attention span or do not behave in the same manner as other types of dog. Yet they certainly can be taught to retrieve and can become fairly competent retrievers.

There are two schools of thought concerning the teaching of a dog to retrieve. The first school believes that retrieving is a fun activity for the dog and owner and should therefore be taught as such. The second school of thought states that retrieving should be force-taught so that the dog isn't allowed to decide that on certain days it will retrieve and on other days it will not. Many professional dog-trainers believe in this approach. If skills are learned naturally they can be lost naturally and hence retrieving must be 'taught' whether or not the dog shows a natural inclination to return any object to hand on command. However, while I confess I am reluctant to force-train any dog of my own – and I've never had need to do so anyway – I admit that should I decide to 'trial dogs' at either the field trial level in which gundogs take part, obedience tests, or the more complex but perhaps less stringent CD, UD, TD, PD test (companion dog, utility dog, tracker dog and police dog), when it is imperative that the dog retrieves an object to hand promptly and without question, I might well adopt one of the force-training methods. However, while I shall mention the force-training methods, the pet dog trainer should endeavour to train his or her puppy by fun-training methods, unless the dog is required to perform in some form of competitive event.

Most puppies show an interest in carrying certain objects, particularly if those objects are pleasant to 'mouth'. Paper, that makes a crinkling sound, is readily mouthed by a young puppy, as is a furry or soft-textured object such as an old glove or an old carpet slipper. There are always certain objects puppies are seen to carry regularly, obviously objects the puppy finds pleasurable to mouth – and these are the objects I usually use to start a puppy retrieving. A puppy scarcely out of the nest will usually chase after and pick up a paper ball rolled in front of it. Once the ball is mouthed, I fall to my hands and knees in front of the whelp so that my face is level with that of the puppy and speak softly to it as it comes towards me with the ball in its mouth (I have mentioned how readily dogs will approach a person who puts his face at the same level as theirs).

The puppy may be reluctant to give up the rolled-up ball, but will usually drop the paper ball if it is given praise or affection. Should a puppy simply take the paper ball to a spot where it can chew the object in peace, I once again fall to my hands and knees and make gentle placatory sounds to entice the puppy to come towards me and give up its paper ball. However, I have found that a noisy or excessive degree of placatory noises will usually ensure that the puppy comes to hand quickly, but leaves its ball behind it. Should that happen, and it often will during the early stages of teaching a puppy to retrieve by this method, I fetch the ball, make a display of pleasure at its recovery and of possessing the object, show the ball to the puppy, throw it once again, and fall to my knees to receive the ball should the puppy bring the object to hand. Quite obviously anyone watching the spectacle would think I was completely mad, so once again I avoid a training session at a spot where people can observe such apparently absurd antics. I usually start retrieving training in an empty room in my home, which must be free of people and, above all, other dogs and small children.

If I cannot find a suitable place to teach a young puppy to retrieve I desist from training until the room is vacant, for to start where people or dogs are present is decidedly counterproductive and produces bad habits that are difficult to eradicate. The very act of retrieving should indicate to the thinking person that the presence of another dog will ruin a retrieving session.

The fact that the puppy runs to the object that has been thrown, mouths the object and carries it about, indicates that the puppy finds the object desirable. Thus it is all the more remarkable that the puppy is willing to carry back the object and relinquish it to the handler in exchange for either a display of profuse affection, or titbits. Should another dog be present in the training area the puppy may well jealously guard its prize, and should that other dog attempt to take the treasured paper ball or dummy, the puppy will usually run off to conceal it. Few dogs actually enjoy retrieving if there is a likelihood of the object they are in the act of fetching to hand being confiscated or even investigated by another dog.

In no type of dog is this retrieving jealousy more manifest than in sight hounds. A greyhound that will catch and retrieve its quarry to hand readily and enthusiastically will usually be less enthusiastic about retrieving if its handler is holding another dog on a slip. In fact the majority of coursing greyhounds are reluctant retrievers, willing to stand over their catches but unwilling to fetch them to hand, simply because they are so used to their handlers fielding many hounds when out coursing. The lurcher, a greyhound derivative, was once the insignia of the village moocher, a solitary ne'er-do-well, the sort of person only a dog could love, and lurchers once had the reputation of bringing every catch to their owners, seeking out these Autolycus-type figures wherever they might be, eager to deliver the 'swag' to hand. These days non-retrieving lurchers are extremely common and many will start to bring their catch to hand, but suddenly start to circle the handler and refuse to give up their rabbit or hare. It is often said the genetic make-up of the lurcher has been changed and intractable non-retrieving lurchers are bred today. What is more likely is that the type of person who keeps lurchers has changed and the one man and one dog relationship the moocher enjoyed with his cur is not enjoyed by the parties of lurcher buffs who wander the countryside with a dozen or so dogs on slips. In fact, it is small wonder that non-retrieving lurchers are so common today.

I am also reluctant to train in places where children are likely to be present or worse still likely to appear suddenly. Wordsworth was completely wrong when he stated 'the child is father to the man'. Children behave as if they are an entirely different species from the adults into which they grow. Children move more jerkily, move more quickly, are noisier and prove absolutely irresistible to puppies. Few puppies will concentrate on retrieving-training when children are about, and the most carefully planned training session invariably degenerates into bedlam if a child suddenly appears on the scene.

Since the early 1980s it has become particularly dangerous to train a puppy in places children frequent, for such have been the atrocities committed by large dogs, that children are now often warned not to go near any dog. Puppies are for some reason (perhaps young animals find other young animals particularly interesting) attracted to children and should a child become panic-stricken at the sight of an approaching puppy the whelp may well misinterpret this and attempt to engage the child in some sort of game. Other puppies become effusively sycophantic when a child starts screaming or display some manifestation of fear and grovel at the feet of the child. The result is a far from vicious circle perhaps, but as the child becomes more and more terrified the puppy becomes even more attentive or submissive. The majority of children or adults attacked by dogs unintentionally provoked the attack after being approached by a dog which manifested no obvious animosity towards them. An obvious display of fear – and dogs have lived in a symbiotic relationship with man for long enough to be able to detect any mannerisms that indicate a person is afraid of them – prompts a dog to attack. I have deliberately avoided any mention of how to teach a dog to attack a person or another animal throughout the book – the attack mechanism is easily turned on, but oh-so-difficult to turn off that I believe guard dog training is best left to professionals. It is nevertheless essential for a dog-owner to know what situations are likely to encourage a dog to attack, so that the trainer can take measures to prevent these situations occurring. Konrad Most, and I shall refer to him later in the book, suggests that the following methods be used to encourage a dog to attack a person. A man or woman approaches the leashed or restrained trained dog and lashes a thin, pliable stick to the right and left of the dog. The dog is alarmed and alerted to the possible danger of the attack and the hurt the attack may engender it. Quite suddenly the attacker feigns fright and attempts to run away. A prey animal attempting to flee arouses the predator's desire to pursue the frightened animal and hence the dog needs little encouragement to attack the now fleeing former antagonist. Many dogs that have little or no desire to attack will in fact seek to investigate a person who is behaving in a terrified manner.

I'm afraid I cannot resist resorting to an anecdote to illustrate a point, and the tale that follows certainly does that. When I lived near Whittington I kept a number of dogs, the barking of which often upset a puppy starting in retrieving-training. Hence I trained near a playing field across which children trudged to school. I keep a particularly sycophantic strain of lurcher, one of the founders of which was a bitch called Fathom. One summer, while retrieving-training during the quiet of an afternoon, a mother and child suddenly appeared at the edge of the field. Fathom became ecstatic and began to attempt to engage the child in play. The child became unusually hysterical and highly vocal, but Fathom interpreted this as an invitation to play. She ran forward rolling on her back in a submissive manner, but the child became more and more upset at the sight of the grovelling, rolling, licking puppy. Her mother was even more upset and suddenly stiffened, falling to the ground and thrashing in a convulsion I misinterpreted as a type of epilepsy. Fathom forsook the child and began to lick the face of the fallen woman (an unintentional pun) who began to thrash and flail all the harder when the puppy stood over her. I ran in, seized and leashed Fathom, while an upset but very sensible husband appeared and explained that his wife was a cynophobe – a person with an unusually strong fear of dogs. What could have been a particularly unpleasant situation was in fact prevented by the husband's calm and sensible attitude, but even afterwards I refrained from training a puppy where children were likely to appear.

To return to retrieving-training, however. Sometimes the puppy will pay little attention to the rolled-up paper ball that was thrown in front of it and approach the most enticing dummy with indifference, sniffing it, but disdaining to mouth the object. This is a particularly common reaction from sight hound puppies, particularly the Middle Eastern sight hounds such as salukis or Afghan hounds. A little thought on the part of the handler will usually produce a method of training to counteract the hound's indifference to stationary objects. My own particular method of encouraging a sight hound puppy to mouth a dummy is to harness the sight hound's desire to chase and to fuse this desire into the retrieving-training programme. I attach the dummy to a length of twine and tow the dummy in front of the whelp, playing the cat and mouse game children are wont to play with kittens, to encourage the sight hound puppy to mouth the moving dummy. Once the puppy has pursued the rolled-up paper ball or the dummy attached to a line, it will usually pick up the dummy if in the middle of an exciting cat and mouse game the dummy with its string attachment is thrown a few yards away. If the puppy refuses to mouth the dummy, a further game of cat and mouse will usually excite the whelp enough to make it want to seize the dummy.

Retrieving-training should be fun for both the dog and the handler and frankly anyone who regards training as an odious chore would be well advised not to keep dogs. Furthermore, retrieving-training should never be continued to a point where the dog becomes bored. In the middle of a game when the puppy is excitedly retrieving the dummy to hand I quit and place the dummy out of reach, leaving the puppy to gaze wistfully up at the place where I placed the dummy. If retrieving-training progresses too long, or the puppy loses interest in the activity, the whelp will find retrieving distasteful and may reject the process of bringing the object to hand. I watch for facial expressions of any dog I am training and when I observe the slightest sign of dismay, boredom or indifference I stop retrieving-training and promptly engage the puppy in a wild romp. In fact a romp should follow any training session, for then the dog comes to associate any aspect of training with the sensation of pleasure.

It is always good sense to vary retrieving-training methods and techniques to prevent boredom. I try to engage puppies in games involving retrieving techniques, hiding objects, sending the puppy to find them, dropping an article *en route* while I walk the whelp and sending the puppy to fetch the article, and various other techniques to prevent a retrieving-training session becoming irksome. If I appear to harp too long on the subject of never letting a retrieving session becoming tedious, I make no apology for doing so.

I began visiting Tom Evan's kennels and helping him with kennel chores shortly after my ninth birthday, but Tom refused to allow me to play with sapling puppies until I was much older lest I ruined the whelps for further training. Like most children, I seldom heeded the advice offered me and one day nearly ruined a litter brother of that famous duo Pinehawk Sark and Pinehawk Spur – dogs that appear in the tails of most top grade springer spaniel lines. I had spent a morning cavorting with the puppy on the hillside near Tom's kennels and hurling my school cap for the puppy to fetch. Tom had watched me for a minute or two before ordering me to stop lest I soured the whelp of retrieving, but as soon as Tom returned to the house the puppy enticed me into resuming the game of fetching my cap.

Eventually the puppy must have become bored with the game and perhaps showed a little less enthusiasm for the romp, but few thirteen-year-old children are perspicacious enough to notice when a training session has begun to pall on a puppy. Tom, however, was only too aware of the signs. He returned, saw me sitting on thc grass, cap in hand, and the puppy sitting just out of reach with a rather upset expression on its face. Tom exploded in one of the few outbursts of fury I ever witnessed from him. His face went puce and then white and he brought a twitch down on my shoulders with such force that the pain took my breath away. On reflection I can now understand why he lost his temper. Socks (each and every puppy kept back to train was called Socks) had more potential than either Sark or Spur but refused to retrieve until her fourth year and Tom rightly or wrongly blamed me for the spaniel's peculiarities and for the fact that, unlike her brothers, she never became a field trial champion. Since that time I have become extremely vigilant about observing when a puppy is becoming tired of a retrieving-training session.

For some reason most dog-training manuals fail to mention that adult dogs and puppies alike may become bored and disenchanted with the action of retrieving the same dummy during each and every training session – though conversely a dog may display a particular desire to retrieve certain objects – particularly unpleasant and apparently malodorous objects. Should a dog display the slightest indifference to the dummy used in a retrieving game session – and I shall deal with forced retrieving presently – the dummy should be discarded and another dummy or object used to continue the game. Breeds with an inbred propensity to retrieve may well agree to retrieve the self-same dummy or object until the device literally falls to pieces. Sight hound or sight hound derivatives such as lurchers or longdogs soon become disenchanted with a dummy that is used too frequently during training sessions and unless force-trained many sight hounds or lurchers and longdogs will refuse to train with an object that has fallen into disfavour with them. It is in fact a great mistake for any dog-trainer to regard all breeds of dog as simply shape, size and colour varieties of the same animal. Different breeds react very differently to certain training sessions and to expect the same reaction from a saluki as from a spaniel is to court disaster. For this reason the majority of professional dog-trainers, most of whom majored with alsatians or labradors, fight shy of accepting sight hounds, particularly recalcitrant sight hounds that have failed to respond to discipline and training as puppies.

Training sight hounds, lurchers or longdogs to retrieve by fun-training methods often taxes the ingenuity of the trainer and the training scheme requires a great deal of variation and adaptation to teach these hounds to become competent retrievers. The fact is that sight hounds become bored all too easily and like teenage youths who also display the self-same boredom need a great deal of stimulation to snap them out of it. A sight hound may display a relentless total commitment when pursuing its quarry – a saluki may well run a hare for several minutes, seemingly oblivious to the activities taking place on the ground where the course is taking place, yet be unable to concentrate on a lengthy training session. A varied training programme is the secret of training any sight hound or sight hound derivative and it is a fact that greyhound trainers will deliberately seek out new and interesting routes to walk their wards, as hounds walked along the same routes every day 'stale' or condition less well than hounds allowed to see new and more interesting walks.

The same principles must apply to the teaching of retrieving where sight hounds are concerned. A sight hound may well eagerly retrieve a crinkled-up paper ball for several days and suddenly display distaste or lack of interest in the object. It is difficult to rekindle interest in retrieving the object again – though if the hound is allowed to see the paper ball animated by a cat-and-mouse string it may well work – for a while at least. However, once the sight hound displays a lack of interest in the dummy it is required to retrieve, it is bad policy to continue using that particular dummy. At the time of writing I pen a 'Lurcher and Longdog' column for a sporting magazine called *Shooting News* and one of the most commonly asked questions I receive is concerned with retrieving-training. The majority of young lurchers apparently sour of retrieving-training and sicken of the use of the same dummy in a relatively short period of time. The answer to such a problem is a simple one – change the dummy used during the training session. I start retrieving-training a lurcher puppy with a folded strip of paper and graduate to a ball of rolled up newspaper. When the puppy tires of this type of dummy I resort to using a soft rubber ball and when the ball no longer excites the youngster I start to use a rolled-up dried rabbit skin. By the time the whelp has become bored with retrieving a rolled-up rabbit skin, it is usually ready to enter to quarry and will be required to retrieve game it has caught, and game is usually far more exciting than any synthetic dummy a trainer can devise.

Flexibility is all important in the training methods used to train and discipline sight hounds and the glib expression 'a sight hound is like any other breed of dog only more so' always must be borne in mind when training any greyhound dog. Many trainers fight shy of taking on one of these dogs, particularly sight hounds of the Middle-Eastern type, and it might be well to include a quote from Mrs Frank Burger, a trainer of performing dogs who includes a troupe of eight Afghan hounds, one of the most difficult greyhound types to train, in her act. Mrs Burger remarks that Afghan hounds, like most other Middle-Eastern greyhounds, take six or seven times as long to train as do non-sight hound breeds and that one must adapt the training sessions to the whims and caprices of the hounds. Sight hounds are certainly more difficult to train than are other breeds of dog and are more headstrong than most breeds of non-sight hound. Few professional trainers succeed with sight hounds of any sort and John Holmes, whose hounds perform extremely well at agility and obedience events, is successful because of his versatile training programmes.

The subject of forced retrieving-training has been touched on and by now the reader may have developed some interest in what this involves or, more to the point, how it differs from what I have called fun-retrieving methods throughout this chapter. Basically force-retrieving is a form of training used to teach a dog always to retrieve an object when so directed no matter what the mood of the dog or the unpleasant nature of the object it is sent to retrieve. For instance, a police or service dog sent to retrieve a recently fired gun, still reeking of cordite, may find the stench of the burning explosive unpleasant and the taste of the gun uncongenial. Likewise gun dogs are often shy of retrieving pigeons to hand though they may be excellent retrievers of other fur and feathered game. Such animals are invariably taught retrieving by what is known as the force-retrieving method. It is also argued by advocates of this method that all obedience competition dogs should be subjected to this sort of training whether or not they show a great willingness to retrieve naturally – for it is argued that an activity that is developed naturally may well cease naturally when the dog decides it no longer finds the action of retrieving congenial.

I include the force-retrieving method suggested by Konrad Most purely out of interest to the reader for it is now illegal in Britain and many other countries. Most, one of the most astute exponents of Pavlovian training methods, conducted crash courses with recalcitrant, savage and often dangerous large dogs and produced serviceable and reliable police and military dogs from them. It is argued that Most used extreme methods so that he could produce well-trained animals in the shortest period of time and there are well-authenticated records to show that some of Most's dogs would rush into blazing houses to retrieve articles he required them to bring to hand. I will describe Most's methods – and the reader must come to his or her conclusions about them. I repeat, such methods would be unacceptable and illegal in Britain.

Most fitted his dogs with a strong leash and also a spiked collar, the spines of which pointed inward and when the collar was slack simply touched the skin of the dog's neck. A great deal of time and experience ascertained just how tightly the collar should fit. The collar was then twisted forcibly and the spines bit into the tender skin of the dog's neck and throat and not surprisingly the animal opened its mouth to utter a yelp, roar or to bite the person inflicting such an outrage on it. Once the mouth was opened a dumb-bell was thrust into the jaws until it touched the gums and lips at the back of the mouth. Immediately the dumb-bell made contact with the lips or the mouth, the pressure on the collar was released at the same moment as the trainer uttered the word 'hold', 'fetch' or its Teutonic equivalent perhaps. This training method has an international flavour about it for it required a trainer with the disposition of a Spanish inquisitor and the reflexes of a Chinese martial arts film star.

The reasoning behind Most's method was decidedly

Pavlovian. The dog was subjected to extreme agony, agony that ceased as soon as the dog grasped the dump-bell or object Most thrust into its mouth. Dogs are hedonists of the first order and hence after a week of this training method apparently raced with great haste to pick up objects thrown for them. This method was lampooned by many and is often referred to as 'Ve have Vays of Making you Fetch', but Most achieved incredible results with his force-training methods – or supposedly so. I have observed this force-training method some three times and each time it reduced the animal concerned to a pitiful wreck. It can be argued that the failures I witnessed may well have been due to the ineptitude of the trainer. However, even if this method was not illegal in Britain, I would advise against its use. I try to encourage the formation of a bond or close relationship between myself and the animals I am endeavouring to train and I cannot but feel that the spiked collar would do little to cement such relationships.

Various other less ferocious methods of force-training are used and I must confess that only three times have I ever had to resort to any form of force-training, and despite the fact that it is not considered either wise or fashionable to fun-train any dog that is required to retrieve without question or compete in competition, I never teach any of my own puppies by force-training methods – and I have never had a fun-trained dog let me down in the field or in any of the competitions I have entered.

The first dog I ever attempted to force-train to retrieve was a springer spaniel sent me by a teaching colleague who enjoyed a temporary interest in rough shooting. My colleague bought a superbly bred dog puppy from one of the best and most reliable strains of field trial springer available – indeed Pinehawk Sark, a dog I had known when he was a puppy, featured in the tail line of the springer's pedigree. Like many tyro springer trainers my associate was of the opinion that all one needed to do to train a gun dog was to take it into a field and let the dog's natural hunting instinct do the rest. It was a fearsome mistake, for springers will often prefer to hunt than eat, and the majority will settle for hunting rather than retrieving. I believe that in the right hands the dog, sired by Hales Smut (a very fashionable sire at that time) would have become a field trial champion. He had drive, courage to face the deepest cover, and a nose the like of which I have seldom seen on any dog. However, like all hunting dogs he needed to have a lengthy period of obedience training before he was introduced to game. Sadly he was never given such obedience training and he came to me eager to hunt up and flush fur or feather and displayed a great willingness to please. Nevertheless he simply refused to retrieve and I strongly suspect that he had been sickened of the practice when he was a puppy. Thus he would give of his best while hunting, give a brief point before flushing game, but he insisted on rushing in, refused to drop to shot and while he would examine shot game he refused to retrieve the game to hand. I agreed to take him on free of charge if my colleague agreed to do my playground duty for a year, read up on the force-training methods – they were at that time referred to as the 'German methods' – and set to with a great deal more enthusiasm than skill to train the dog to retrieve. The force-training method worked moderately well and the dog became a moderate if reluctant retriever. My colleague however obtained promotion at another school, left and never honoured his agreement concerning playground duty. I confess therefore that I had somewhat mixed feelings when a year later I saw that the dog which was seldom given refresher courses in forced retrieving had reverted to its former bad habits and refused to retrieve.

The second animal I was required to teach retrieving by the forced or German method was an imported saluki that had spent its puppyhood incarcerated in a quarantine kennels where it had been lead-trained and given virtually no other training. I was brought the dog when its owner failed to get it to return to hand on command and to use his own words, 'he could do nothing with it'. The saluki showed no inclination to breed – it was purchased as a potential stud dog – and it is my opinion that its lack of socialising and lack of contact with other dogs rendered this one 'strange' and even more remote than even salukis are wont to be. On the credit side, if credit side there be, it would course anything that moved, be it hares, rabbits, sheep, cattle or scraps of paper shifted by the wind, yet once it laid low its prey or realised the object of its attentions was inanimate it simply stood over its catch until its interest waned. It then either ambled aimlessly in the direction of the owner, circling him but refusing to be caught up or sought other quarry to course. In short it became a nightmare to own and, as I professed to specialise in the training of recalcitrant sight hounds, I was brought the beast for training and wonder of wonders by dint of the German method or force-retrieving I taught the animal not only to pick up and carry its catch but to return the catch to hand. I have never known a more grateful customer than the owner of the dog. I was paid handsomely for my work and each Christmas sent snapshots of the saluki carrying to hand. However, my experience with the owner of the third dog I force-trained was a little less than pleasant.

Shortly after the first Lambourn Lurcher Show in 1974 it became extremely fashionable to own a lurcher and it was by no means uncommon to see long, lean greyhoundy dogs in the backs of expensive cars, whereas a decade or so ago the lurcher was the hallmark of the rural disreputable, the poacher or the rustic Autolycus figure. Any rough-coated lurcher of dubious origin was advertised as a deerhound greyhound and found a ready market amongst the social group that liked to consider themselves as 'nouveau rustics'. Most of these dogs received no formal training other than to be lead-trained and slipped at the odd hare as the dog and owner walked the fields. I was seldom offered lurchers to train partly because the majority of owners expected little of their dogs and partly because the average lurcher could be bought for a song, sold for roughly the same price when ruined by inadequate training and the lot of most lurchers became pitiable. In 1978 I was sent one lurcher to train, an adult near greyhound-type lurcher that was as recalcitrant as a saluki and neither hunted nor came to hand. It was in fact the most inert animal I have ever trained and proved a test of all my ingenuity and patience. I accepted the dog on the agreement that I was paid a fixed weekly price which was slightly more than a boarding kennel would have charged to house the dog, and the dog spent some six months in my care. It learned to retrieve, come to hand smartly and even hunt up game after a fashion, but when I persuaded the owner to fetch the dog he declined to pay me stating that he'd 'see me right' – a dubious sort of promise at the best of times. He never did 'see me right' and promptly sold the dog for £40. Since that date I have been reluctant to accept any lurcher for training and the majority of trainers can tell similar tales of lurchers left in their kennels for months only to be sold by a somewhat less than interested owner who was reluctant to pay the trainer's fees. Enough, however of my bleats concerning the frailties of lurcher owners except to say that it is modern practice for most trainers to train the owner as well as the dog and for this reason dog training videos are becoming more and more popular with tyro dog owners.

Force-training too relies on the fact that the majority of dogs delight in pleasing their owner or trainer, but no one should attempt to force-train a dog unless that dog has undergone a programme of training which has made it reasonably obedient. It is in fact virtually impossible to force-train a dog that is actively struggling to get away from the trainer – and at this point it also fair to mention that it is extremely difficult to force-train a dog that is suspicious or frightened of the trainer. Thus any trainer taking on a new dog with a view to schooling it at force-retrieving should develop a relationship with the dog and ascertain just how obedient the dog is before subjecting it to the forced training programme. I write from bitter experience – my attempt to force-train a saluki straight out of quarantine and suspicious of everyone and everything was at first very unsuccessful until the dog learned to come to hand and lost its fear of me.

It is always wise to begin a force-training session with the dog on the lead, for when an animal is subjected to a baffling and sometimes distressing experience, it may well decide to 'cut and run' and the training schedule takes several backward steps when this happens. When the dog is secured I put the animal at the sit position and with my hand across the top of the muzzle gently squeeze the lips against the dog's gums. This action causes the dog to open its mouth and the trainer should now insert the dumb-bell or dummy in the animal's mouth and utter the command 'hold' or 'take' or 'fetch' – or any other command the trainer intends to use throughout the training programme.

Each dog's reaction to this apparent indignity will be slightly different. Some dogs will actively spit out the dumb-bell or dummy as if it has a disagreeable taste. Others will freeze, dumb-bell in mouth, as if petrified by the experience, with a look on their faces that suggests they expected far worse to come. However, no matter how the trainer does it he must make sure the dog holds the dumb-bell in its mouth – though once again extreme hurt or fear engendered by the training session is most decidedly counter-productive. All the time while this training method is proceeding the trainer should continue to repeat the command 'hold' or 'fetch' or 'carry' while holding the jaws of the dog shut to prevent it dropping the dumb-bell.

When the dog does condescend to hold the dumb-bell in his jaws, the trainer must now praise the dog enthusiastically and then very gently remove the dumb-bell while uttering the command 'give' or 'drop it' or 'release'. It is worth noting that the tyro dog-trainer attempting to train his or her first dog may well vary the commands uttering 'fetch' one day and 'hold' the next. This in fact is a very bad practice and thoroughly confusing for the dog. More experienced dog-trainers develop a repertoire of commands and seldom if ever vary them. Tom Evans, the springer spaniel breeder with whom I served my dog-training apprenticeship, always uttered the Welsh word 'diolch' (thank you) when he wished the puppy to give up its catch. He had never varied his praise word in all the years he trained spaniels and went to his grave using the self-same command. When he sold a part-trained puppy or a grown dog it involved the owner taking a crash course in Welsh, but years after I had left Wales I watched a field trial on the Borders of Scotland and England and heard a very broad Glaswegian accent attempt the word 'diolch'. I knew instantly who had bred the young springer bringing its catch to hand.

I am invariably asked as to just how long an average dog takes to learn to hold a dummy between its jaws during a force-training session. The answer of course must be that there is no average dog – at least as far as the subject of force-training is concerned. I have attended numerous courses where this exercise was taught to students and the instructor used a variety of breeds to demonstrate the training method. Frankly, there seems to be no correlation between the breed to be taught the skill and the length of time needed to teach a dog the technique. I have however observed that some trainers are amazingly adept at teaching the skill while others are less so – and while I confess I am a confirmed middle-aged sexist, I must admit some of the most efficient exponents of force-retrieving training are women.

However, satisfying as the sight of a dog holding a bar, dumb-bell or dummy in its mouth on the command of 'hold', 'fetch' or 'carry' might be (and I have found it to be extremely satisfying when I failed to train animals by the natural retrieving method) the exercise must progress if the dog is to be taught to fetch certain objects to hand on command. The trainer must now proceed with the deliberate and calculated, careful slowness that would delight an austringer training a goshawk. The dummy or dumb-bell must be held gently against the dog's lips and pressed gently against the mouth while the command 'fetch', 'carry' or 'hold' is uttered and in all probability the dog will open its mouth in anticipation and the dumb-bell is gently thrust into the mouth. More often than not the dog will attempt to lick the dumb-bell rather than seize it and even this gesture must be praised by the handler, though not so effusively as to excite the dog and break the training session, but it is only a matter of time before even the most stubbornly obdurate dog will open its mouth to take the dummy.

It is superfluous to advise the trainer to show pleasure at the sight of the dog seizing the dummy for the exhilaration the trainer experiences at this first triumphal step at force-training will be hard to conceal. Nor should he conceal his pleasure at the dog's success. In fact, so excited will the typical trainer become at this first small success that the excitement will certainly infect the dog and at this stage I would advise stopping the training session and engaging the dog in a wild excited game and not to return to force-training lessons for the rest of the day or at least for several hours. It would in fact be fascinating to watch the face of a disinterested observer watching the exultation and delight this first successful step in forced retrieving inspires in the trainer for even if forced retrieving gives the dog little pleasure in its initial training stages the success of the training session gives the trainer an enormous lift. I can well remember when I achieved my first success at forced retrieving and having to steel myself to tell total strangers of my triumph and be regarded as a certifiable lunatic.

As with an austringer training a hawk, the object the dog is to seize must be held slightly further from the dog's jaws at each successive lesson and the trainer must accept that he may experience the occasional 'blip' on the training programme when the dog is no longer able to stretch its neck to fetch the object and must leave the 'sit' position to fetch the dummy. Some dogs will refuse to lift themselves to the stand position to pick up the dummy and the trainer must then gently encourage the dog to stand and move forward to pick up the dummy that is held a yard or so from its face.

The reader may have noticed that I have advised the trainer to continue holding the dummy and not to cast it on the ground before the dog. Some dogs find it acceptable to take the dummy from the trainer's hands but are reluctant to pick it up from the floor. My forced training sessions with the saluki dog I have mentioned had progressed wonderfully well and with very few hiccoughs until I threw the dumb-bell on the ground and uttered the 'fetch' command. To my amazement my ward gazed at me with the bewildered, bored stare that only a saluki can seem to generate and I confess I was baffled at his indifference. I engaged the dog in a wild, exciting game and went back to the force-training session only to find the dog still found the action of picking up the dummy from the floor just as bewildering as before.

I cannot resist relating the anecdote of how I overcame this problem. At that time my interest in collecting Jack London's books and articles had brought me into contact with Frank Cutler Jones, a fellow collector and circus artist who swallowed swords and performed under the pseudonym of 'The Great Polanski' – a name he decided to drop when the producer/director Roman Polanski became involved in a spot of paedophilic scandal. Frank was, to use his own expression, from 'carny stock' and became a sword-swallower when his father, also a Polanksi, performed a dare-devil's stunt of *swallowing* a neon tube and lighting up the tube stationed inside his stomach, and oesophagus. One night the tube smashed and Polanski senior died of peritonitis leaving Frank or Polanski junior to forsake his strongman act and his role of stooge for white-faced clowns, to become a sword-swallower.

Frank had in his time worked with the Hoi sisters, two diminutive Goldi women from central Asia who taught a variety of animals from pigs to borzois to perform amazing feats at the Russian state circuses – and I make no apologies for the fact that this chapter has taken on the aura of a George Burns soliloquy. What is more Frank had a film of the Hoi sisters teaching a variety of very tiny poodle-like dogs to retrieve using the 'German' method. Contrary to the plots of Len Deighton novels, I have had no difficulty obtaining films, books or scientific data from behind the Iron Curtain – far less difficulty than I have had obtaining similar data from Scottish Universities, I should add. The film of the Hoi sisters played to the background music of Mussorgsky's 'Pictures At An Exhibition' showed forced retrieving training at its very best and the youngest sister simply eased the dog's head to the fallen dumb-bell, in time with 'Pictures' one should add, uttering the Russian equivalent of 'fetch', 'take' or 'carry' and in minutes the poodle-like mites were retrieving any object.

In short, I returned to my saluki training session with a new heart, undertook a quick refresher course with the animal, for salukis forget so easily and, to the rhythmic music of Mussorgsky ringing in my ears, forced the saluki's head gently to the dummy uttering the word 'fetch'. The dog picked up the dumb-bell first time and henceforth whenever I was asked to demonstrate force-retrieving methods to a lurcher club, I could not perform unless I heard the music of 'Pictures At An Exhibition'. I became quite proficient at force-retrieving, though never as skilful as those olive-skinned Hoi sisters. Circus dog-trainers are in a class of their own.

Once the dog acquires the skill of stepping forward a short distance to pick up the dumb-bell or dummy, the trainer is home and dry, so to speak, and henceforth the training session is simply a matter of progression. Each and every success on the part of the dog must however always be rewarded by the use of titbits and/or effusive praise and the jubilation experienced by the trainer should always spill over and infect the dog. The diminutive Hoi twins became ecstatic (to the strains of Mussorgsky) when their animals progressed from one training session to another.

It is a mistake, I believe, to break the euphoria of initial retrieving training with the slightest element of restraint – for instance, placing the dog at the sit position and allowing it to pursue and fetch the dummy only when the owner decides it should do so. True, it is essential to teach the dog restraint, but never in the initial training programme, when the dog should be excited by its performance and its excitement should never be dulled by the owner attempting to restrain the activity by requiring the dog to sit or lie while engaged in a retrieving game. Once again the William James epigram should come to mind: 'The essential difference between play and work lies not in the nature of the activity itself but in the attitude of the doer towards it'.

Many dogs, particularly ecstatic and enthusiastic retrievers

– and some dogs are obsessive retrievers – will race out, grab the dummy, flash back nearly to hand and promptly *drop* the dummy before retrieving it to the trainer's hand. Now, to the pet dog owner this is not a serious fault (and it is certainly not as irritating as the practice of a dog that races after the object thrown and careers around holding the object in its mouth but making no attempt to return it to the trainer – I have dealt with this problem earlier). However, the retriever that brings its prize almost to hand but insists on dropping the object near the trainer's feet can be an unmitigated nuisance if the dog is a gun dog or worse still a very soft-mouthed lurcher. Dogs required to return shot or caught game to hand but who persist in dropping the catch near the trainer's feet can be a great nuisance – 'winged' birds (shot but not killed) will promptly stagger off before the handler can bag them. Worse still is the very soft-mouthed lurcher that insists on dropping a rabbit or hare near its owner's feet, for the quarry, scarcely incapacitated by being caught, promptly hightails it away from the dog and handler and often succeeds in escaping.

One of the foundation males of my strain of lurcher was a tall, powerfully built animal who in addition to being an outstanding athlete displayed a curious sense of fun – a quality as near to a sense of humour as a dog could possess. He caught rabbits easily, scarcely altering his stride as he did so but as he presented them to hand he dropped them and allowed them to run a short distance before he recaught them. I allowed the peculiarity to manifest and possibly correct itself a few times and finally stopped the idiosyncrasy by subjecting the dog to a crash retraining course uttering 'hold' or 'carry' as he approached with the dummy and only taking the dummy from him when he brought it exactly to hand.

Dogs which, while carrying the dummy, refuse to approach the handler can be encouraged to do so if the handler drops to a crouch position with his face level with that of the dog, but even this method is not always effective. Other methods of making the dog bring its catch to hand are numerous and one of the most efficacious ways of bringing the circling dog carrying a dummy in its jaws to hand is to turn one's back on the animal and promptly walk away, ignoring the dog. Most dogs cannot tolerate this type of rejection and follow the owner, often staying very close to heel. The handler is therefore able to turn and take the dummy from the dog. It is amazing how many even very dominant dogs cannot stand rejection and promptly apparently mend their ways when it appears that the handler is ignoring them. Middle Eastern sight hounds such as Afghan hounds, sloughis and salukis are perhaps more resistant to experiencing discomfort when ignored or simply rejected and this should always be borne in mind when the trainer walks away from the circling hound in fields which may harbour a strong game scent. I confess I have made many mistakes when I have credited such hounds with having the idiosyncrasies of other breeds of dog. Any dog-trainer who does not admit to having made fairly serious errors while training any breed of dog is stretching the truth more than just a little.

Retrieving should be a fun event. It should be fun for the dog to learn, it should be fun for the trainer to teach and if possible should be taught as a fun activity – as an exciting game. I confess I still experience a childlike delight in teaching a young puppy to retrieve, and in this respect I pray that I shall never lose my Peter Pan attitude to training a puppy.

14

A Question of Punishment

During my third year in teaching I took up an appointment in a very rough ghetto and as Johnny-Come-Lately I was given a class of very violent remedials many of whom later achieved star billing in the *Police Gazette*. As the term approached the Christmas break, a young, bespectacled academic arrived to sit out the fury of his probationary year. He was promptly set on by the senior boys, beaten, kicked and floored most days and sexually assaulted by the middle school girls. He survived, well, just survived, by dint of dogged determination though his classes were bedlam, his discipline non-existent, and his way with children poor, to say the least. At the end of the year he left the school and took up a post of an educational psychologist – advising teachers on problem children and how to overcome discipline difficulties. His career was by no means unique, and many teachers hold educational psychologists in very low regard simply because these teachers are aware that their advisors are failed didactics.

The majority of dog-trainers regard the now oh-so-popular dog psychologists (behaviourists who have set up in business advising people on how to control disturbed dogs) in the same light as teachers regard educational psychologists. Edwin Judd, a one-time police dog-handler and rottweiler devotee, sums up this opinion succinctly: 'Show me just one dog psychologist with a well-trained dog.' However to dismiss the findings of every psychologist, both educational and canine researcher, as simply bunkum is to say the least unwise, but once again I urge the reader to practise commonsense rather than to slavishly adhere to the findings of some psychologist whose PhD was praised and lauded by other academics who may be equally out of step with reality. Good, sound, clear thinking preceded academia by millenia and an ounce of commonsense is worth a ton of scientific data. Frederick the Second knew all about imprinting in animals and birds long before Tinbergen penned his Nobel Prize-winning paper on the subject and furthermore The Stupor Mundi knew how to exploit and use this peculiarity when it manifested itself in his falcons. Trainers of desert hounds, skilled in their art long before Abraham Ur of the Chaldees, knew all about gradual and progressive entering of their hounds thousands of years before Skinner and as Rudolph Steiner once said, 'Modern science often only rediscovers ancient knowledge'.

I've taken a long-winded run-up to the subject of punishing a dog, but I make no apology for doing so – a commonsense approach to the subject of punishment is worth a dozen papers by Eysenck – and I honestly believe Eysenck would have agreed with me regarding my last statement. Take for instance the warning note of an irate mother who seeing her offspring committing a misdeed shouts, 'Wait until your father gets home' and the child, dreading the return of the father, contemplates the nature of the offence and the anxiety engendered as time passes makes the punishment for the crime tenfold. Likewise, a headmaster dealing with an academic child who has committed an only moderately severe offence will often make the child wait an hour or so outside the headmaster's office before punishing the miscreant – for the waiting is far more terrifying than the most savage corporal punishment.

Not so with dogs, I'm afraid. Dogs have low attention spans and need to be punished as they are committing or immediately after they have committed a crime, misdeed or rather an antisocial act would seem a more appropriate expression. Once more I shall resort to an anecdote to illustrate a point. I hunted a terrier pack of between thirty to sixty terriers for some twenty-three years and the pack were totally steady to sheep, cattle, poultry, ferrets and other farm livestock. Only one terrier actually failed to be trained to be broken to the livestock amongst which we hunted – a bitch called Climber, a good-natured animal where people were concerned and one of the finest hunting dogs I have ever bred – were it not for her propensity to kill any livestock she encountered. Climber had been savagely punished – it is often difficult to restrain one's emotions when a dog creates havoc on one's beloved livestock, yet seconds after she wreaked havoc on my Leghorn pullets she would endeavour to engage me in play as if she had never perpetrated the misdeed. If a dog commits a misdeed it must be punished within a second or so of committing it and the punishment never perpetrated once the owner has taken the dog home. It is all too easy to delay punishment when the dog commits misdeed in a public place. The general public are decidedly antipathetic to the sight of a mother smacking a child's leg or an owner chastising a dog but if a child commits a misdeed or a dog misbehaves the most efficacious time to punish either is immediately after they have offended. The 'wait till your father gets home' attitude is quite useless in the case of dogs, or in the case of very young children, for that matter.

Yet the most heinous fault in dog-training is regularly witnessed in most public places. It is fairly safe to say that the majority of pet dogs are woefully badly behaved and those of the general public who are decidedly antipathetic to dogs are correct in saying few dogs should be left on the leash. I ask the reader to cast his or her mind back to the last time he or she witnessed a pet dog owner, dog tugging on lead, turn the dog loose in a public place. The dog runs itself into a state of excitement and exhilaration and if there are other dogs present invariably engages the other dog in a wild game. Owners, however, usually tire of watching the game long before the dogs decide they are ready to quit and hereafter follows a ritual that is as predictable as a Catholic Mass. The owner calls his pet, who unless the dog is well and truly trained, is disinclined to break off the game and return to hand. The owner then resorts to a display of histrionics and insists in a loud voice that the dog comes instantly to hand. The dog does not find the tone too persuasive. Indeed it is threatened by the histrionic display and the angry voice and hence continues its game albeit a shade less enthusiastically for it is frightened by the voice and gestures manifested by its owner. The owner is embarrassed and a) shouts the louder and gesticulates even more furiously or b) tries a placatory tone, crouching and sweet talking the animal which may eventually come to hand whereupon the owner berates or chastises the bewildered animal before placing it on the lead and dragging it home only too aware that the dog has made its handler look a fool – and incidentally one suspects that as soon as the dog arrives home it can expect a further reminder of its misdeeds! Wild dogs must be incredibly stupid animals – they must be, to desire a symbiotic relationship with a creature as illogical as man.

To return to that much abused creature the educational psychologist a moment, most will instruct the teacher that certain aspects of his or her class control method are out of kilter and then like phantoms steal away without advising the teacher how to correct those problems. I shall endeavour not to fall into this trap so here is how I would cope with the situation I've just described. First, if the dog I was leading was not particularly well trained or worse still a young puppy, I'd be careful about releasing the dog in a wide open space or worse still in a wide open space where other dogs were playing. If I turned the animal loose in such a situation I should expect the dog to indulge in a fairly lengthy game and sit back and let matters take their course rather than run around attempting to get the dog to come to hand and making a fool out of myself in the process.

When the fervour of the game had abated slightly I would

turn my back on my dog and appear to walk away, always keeping a weather eye on the dog lest the animal found new interests and ran off to engage in yet another game. When the dog condescended to follow me I would crouch, call the dog to me and make a great fuss of the animal when it came to hand – if necessary concealing the fury I may have felt at being inconvenienced by the dog's misdemeanour. Only after I had indulged the dog in a fairly lengthy display of exaggerated affection and praise would I put the animal on a choke chain and take it home.

Now to explain my actions and to explain why the behaviour of the irate dog owner was illogical. First, I would have realised that the excitement engendered in a puppy when it met a whelp of a like age would make the puppy almost impossible to call to hand until it had burned out its initial enthusiasm for the games the pair were likely to play and I would not have wasted my energy either calling or gesticulating to the whelp. I would never have tried to chase after the whelp – for I've yet to meet the dog I can outrun and the sight of a grown person chasing a dog makes an adult look really foolish – and very very angry because he too eventually realises the futility of his actions. I would walk away once the game had run its course simply because dogs are basically pack animals and prefer to stay with a familiar pack – namely me – and hence would be most likely to follow me than to follow the other dog. Please don't take this pack behaviour technique too far, however – I'll explain why later. When the whelp does come to hand, a savage chastising certainly isn't what it needs – the creature doesn't feel it has done wrong – it hasn't, it has simply engaged in games that are an essential part of canine adolescent behaviour (and puppies not allowed to engage in the games grow into rather strange adult dogs) so the fuss and praise I've lavished on him before placing him on the chain (which few dogs enjoy) would make him aware of how pleasurable it was to return to hand – and the chain would be slipped on only when the dog had exulted in the effusive praise I had given him.

For the tops in whacko quasi canine pseudo-psychology

however, one would be hard pushed to find anything more ludicrous than the notion that a dog should only be chastised with a rolled-up length of newspaper – the theory being that the noise of the paper being brought down on the whelp terrified the puppy but inflicted no actual physical hurt on it. Shortly after World War II psychologists no longer engaged in studying combat fatigue and shell shock, turned their attention to child development or methods of modifying canine behaviour and promptly made a pig's ear out of writing reams of what can only be described as pseudo-scientific hokum. A craze which advocated never stopping children doing virtually anything they pleased produced such a set of maladjusted wretches as to fill the Albert Hall let alone an A.S. Neil establishment and a batch of theories concerning canine behaviour that read like the text of an Edward Lear book. Whacking a dog with a rolled-up newspaper was deemed to be good while a smack across the dog's rump with the palm of one's hand was considered an entirely unsuitable punishment for the animal – no matter what misdeed the dog had committed.

Let's hold such theories up to the cold light of reason – a light that seldom penetrates the darkness of dogdom. Is it any more injurious to the animal to bring a newspaper noisily crashing down on its rump than to deliver a swift but not too heavy slap with the palm of the hand across the self-same rump? Furthermore, fewer misdeeds are likely to be committed in a household than are likely to be committed when the dog is being trained out of doors or running free. Hence the trainer must carry a rolled-up newspaper wherever he takes the dog. This is not only totally impractical but most dog-trainers are considered a shade odd by the public at large and the sight of a dog-handler, dog on leash, with rolled-up paper in the other hand would give the impression of a suitable case for treatment running at large.

When dogs have misbehaved I have smacked them with the palm of my hand and still expected them to take food from the same palm. It is absurd to imagine that if a dog is smacked with the palm of the hand he will always regard that palm as a symbol of hostility. May I qualify this statement however for while I have trained (and smacked) many dogs, I have never overdone the punishment or beaten the dog until it is a quivering wreck – though once again I have felt like doing this a hundred times or more in the case of Climber, my one and only failure as a pack terrier. Such a savage thrashing would not only be brutal but rather a pointless waste of human energy – and the action not only reduces the dog to a pitiful wreck, but also demeans the handler in his own eyes, once the temper that has prompted the thrashing has passed.

I find the new cult of the trainer attempting to become a surrogate pack member – essentially an Alpha male in order to train the dog – not only rather silly but just a shade unrealistic – and I'd best explain what I mean before proceeding further. The current trend or fad (call it what you like) amongst dog-trainers is not to treat the dog as one of the family – a bad anthropomorphic notion admittedly – but for the trainer to act as one of the canine pack and to relegate the dog to the correct or appropriate order of peck within the said pack. To a certain extent this is good sound sense – a dog should accept its position as Epsilon member of the family – below that of the very youngest child, and never question its position or try to advance it. Dogs are seldom jealous of the baby – an oft-repeated bleat of those that are tired of and seek for a reason to put down the family pet – I'm afraid they are simply vying with the child for a position within the human pack.

This theory of infiltrating the canine pack in order to train an animal is by no means new. In 1935 Count Max Thun Hohenstein conducted a series of tests concerning the training of monkeys – and primates despite their apparently high intelligence are certainly not the easiest animals to train. He found that monkeys could be subdued or convinced of their lower order of peck if subjected to a quick nip in the shoulder from the trainer, rather than a thrashing from the said gentleman. Fine – and it takes all sorts, I suppose – and

I'm not one who would go out of his way to bite monkeys – but Thun Hohenstein triggered off a whole new line of thought by his one simple experiment, and the conclusions he drew from these tests.

It became fashionable to subdue or punish dogs in the same manner that a canine pack leader would supposedly punish the offender – fine – except perhaps that few of the writers of dog manuals advocating these extraordinary methods had observed the social habits of a pack of wild canids, or for that matter watched the behaviour of a pack of dogs of any sort. For the life of me I cannot see why the currently popular method of punishing a recalcitrant or disobedient dog is to lift the dog clear of the ground by the ruff of its throat and soundly shake it – though this method is reputed to replicate the method used by Alpha canids to punish subordinates. This is totally illogical. During my years of hunting a pack of terriers I never once saw a puppy lifted clear of the ground and shaken. In fact if I might draw on my study of frightening dogs, it is a fact that a dog lifted clear of the ground and shaken is in danger of having its neck dislocated – frequently the case when terriers pick a quarrel with a dog of greater size.

It is however true that dogs are easily frightened by the action of seizing their ruffs, lifting them to the level of the human face and shaking them. Eye contact – I've dealt with this subject when discussing keeping the dog in the 'down' position – plays a certain part in instilling fear in the dog suspended above the ground by its ruff and the fear of falling from the position (a fear common to all mammals) also helps frighten the dog, but to imagine that this technique of punishing a dog imitates the manner in which an Alpha male punishes a lesser pack member is rubbish and totally illogical rubbish at that. It should also be pointed out that while it is relatively easy to lift and chastise a terrier-sized dog, performing the same exercise with a dog the size of a mastiff, a St Bernard or a Great Dane becomes a feat to tax a Hercules rather than the average pet-owner. An Alpha canid wishing to punish or frighten a subordinate simply shoulder charges its victim, nips the victim around the head, face or neck while doing so and stands astride its victim snarling or threatening to bite.

A fact that the majority of dog psychologists, behaviourists, call them what you will, seem to overlook is that man has only recently attempted to infiltrate into the social structure of the canid pack. Yet dogs have, at least according to Dembeck, infiltrated into the social structure of the human family for perhaps as long as 100,000 years. Few behaviourists will accept that dogs will have undergone some social metamorphosis through their lengthy symbiotic relationship with man. Dogs not only accept but understand some of the idiosyncrasies of human behaviour for they have adjusted until they have blended into the ways of men. They understand that a smack or blow indicates human displeasure at some action or misdeed they have committed, and there is little need for misguided humans to attempt to infiltrate into the social structure of domesticated canids. It is said that the Crisler family who domesticated and after a fashion trained Alaskan wolves needed to fit into the social structure of a mini wolf pack in order to be able to live alongside their wards. Yet even after a single generation the Crislers observed that the wolves were blending into the structure of the human family. Ten thousand or so generations of domestication may not have destroyed the canine pack structure or drastically altered the way canids behave, but it will certainly have ameliorated canine behaviour.

By all means read up on the behaviour of wild or primitive canids. I recommend Lopez's *Of Wolves and Men* or Riddle's *The Wild Dogs in Life and Legend*. Both make fascinating reading, both give an interesting insight into the way wild dogs behave, hunt and breed. However, for the reader to imagine that by studying the behaviour of wild canids, he or she will learn how to train the fireside family pet is little short of ludicrous.

Lorenz, one of the few behaviourists who seem to be able to pen a readable book, makes an interesting point concerning how different dogs react to punishment. In his compelling though scarcely accurate book *Man Meets Dog* he makes a pertinent point regarding punishment tailored not so much to fit the crime but to suit the temperament of individual dogs. An incident had prompted Lorenz to chastise both his German shepherd dog bitches, a rather dominant ebullient bitch Stasi, and her subservient daughter Pygi. Both had in fact set about a passing Maltese terrier with the speed with which only German shepherd dog owners realise their dogs are capable. Lorenz pulled the pair off the luckless Maltese which was fortunately still alive and while he mildly chastised the more submissive Pygi, he soundly thrashed the more dominant Stasi. Onlookers criticised Lorenz, not for thrashing his dogs, but for what to them seemed a totally unfair system of punishments – but then non-dog owners are invariably anthropomorphic in their attitude towards dog training and seldom see sound sense in dog-training methods.

Had Lorenz sought to take revenge on his dogs for the sin of attacking the terrier and the humiliation the act caused him, then it would seem fairly logical to set about each bitch with equal severity. Lorenz however had punished his dogs in the hope (and alas he was probably mistaken) that the beatings would deter further attacks on small dogs. Stasi needed firm handling to convince her of the error of her ways and hence Lorenz thrashed her savagely. Pygi, a more submissive animal, needed less firm handling to ensure she would desist from attacking small dogs and indeed the thrashing given to her mother would have mentally damaged the less dominant bitch. Will Humphreys, who in addition to being a great falconer and trainer of Llewellyn setters was also Lord of the Manor of Ratlinghope and Stretton in the Dale, took Lorenz's logic one step further. If two or more setters offended him he thrashed the dominant setter first and allowed the less dominant ones to watch the chastisement for their terror at seeing their litter mate thrashed was often enough to deter them from further misdeeds. Humphreys was considered by many to be the last bastion of the old school of dog-training, but in many ways his methods were decidedly *avant garde* – and always well thought out.

If a headmaster of a public school found two of his wards guilty of some offence and dished out six of the best to one and a single stroke to the other he would be considered unfair (and probably unemployed if he attempted this chastisement in a modern comprehensive school) but his actions would be scientifically sound if one lad was rebellious and his accomplice a shy retiring lad (modern educational thinking suggests that punishment of any sort is a pointless exercise, one should add). However, if a kennel man was to punish all his wards with equal severity many of his dogs would display fearsome neurosis in and out of kennels.

I can't resist the use of an anecdote to further illustrate the point. Merab, my best lurcher, and her granddaughter Phaedra are so similar as to be difficult to tell apart, yet two more different dogs have yet to be born to the strain. Merab is one of the most submissive, sycophantic animals I've ever owned – a joy to train, eager to please and so easily restrained. Phaedra is rebellious, hard-headed, wilful and added to this has the most incredible nose – and a strong-willed dog with an excellent nose is a trainer's nightmare. Last season when the fields around my house were so waterlogged that sheep could not graze on the lower pastures both bitches crawled along a water ditch into a field, and coursed and caught a hare that was unable to run at its best because of the muddy ground. The event was the highlight of their lives for both had been previously outclassed by the sheer speed of strong hares.

Once the fields dried and lambs were pastured on the paddocks it no longer became expedient to allow the dogs to hunt the pastures, yet the excitement generated by their one and only successful course and catch has never been forgotten. As we pass the water ditch along which the dogs found entry to the field, both check the banks for scent. Merab returns at the click of my fingers but if I lose eye control on Phaedra she is into the ditch and through to the field in seconds. Merab needed no punishment to convince her the field was now *verboten*. Phaedra still needs a sharp short warning shout as she approaches the gap. It would be impracticable to punish both in a similar way as indeed it would be unreasonable to attempt to train both by exactly the same methods.

On now to what is considered to be a hot potato amongst dog handlers, namely controlling or punishing a dog from a distance and lest this statement seems a little like a theme from a Star Trek episode I shall explain forthwith. It is easy or relatively easy to discipline a rebellious dog when the said dog is on a leash. It is less easy to discipline that selfsame dog when it is running free of the leash and desirous of committing an antisocial act. Most in his now highly controversial book *Dog Training* advises the use of a special throwing stick to punish the recalcitrant free-running dog. This stick consisted of a handle and a weighted head – and while I believe these throwing sticks certainly stop a disobedient dog dead in its tracks, dead may well be the operative word, for twice I have seen dogs knocked unconscious when the handler has misjudged his aim. Most's methods were invariably harsh, but so also were the adaptations of Most's techniques.

Shortly after my twelfth birthday I spent my Saturdays picking acorns which I sold to a local gun dog trainer for 1¼d per pound. It was easy work and I have no complaint about the payment. The trainer used the acorns as missiles for a catapult and shot them with almost unfailing accuracy at a springer spaniel that displayed a tendency to 'run in' – a cardinal fault in a gun dog of this type. Tom Evans, my mentor, disagreed with this method of bringing a runner to its senses and once when I was engaged in some activity near the rugby field that adjoined Tom's kennel he deliberately fired an acorn at my naked back. The pain was excruciating and the acorn raised a six inch bruise on my lumbar region. Tom was undismayed at my pain and simply uttered, 'Old ——'s springers were just as thin-coated as you are and the impact would have had much the same effect.' It is doubtful that Tom, – a dustbin man by trade, would ever have heard of Rousseau, but he possessed a strange inborn wisdom that her the field was now *verboten*. Phaedra still needs a sharp short warning shout as she approaches the gap. It would be impracticable to punish both in a similar way as indeed it would be unreasonable to attempt to train both by exactly the same methods.

On now to what is considered to be a hot potato amongst dog handlers, namely controlling or punishing a dog from a distance and lest this statement seems a little like a theme from a Star Trek episode I shall explain forthwith. It is easy or relatively easy to discipline a rebellious dog when the said dog is on a leash. It is less easy to discipline that selfsame dog when it is running free of the leash and desirous of committing an antisocial act. Most in his now highly controversial book *Dog Training* advises the use of a special throwing stick to punish the recalcitrant free-running dog. This stick consisted of a handle and a weighted head – and while I believe these throwing sticks certainly stop a disobedient dog dead in its tracks, dead may well be the operative word, for twice I have seen dogs knocked unconscious when the handler has misjudged his aim. Most's methods were invariably harsh, but so also were the adaptations of Most's techniques.

Shortly after my twelfth birthday I spent my Saturdays picking acorns which I sold to a local gun dog trainer for 1¼d per pound. It was easy work and I have no complaint about the payment. The trainer used the acorns as missiles for a catapult and shot them with almost unfailing accuracy at a springer spaniel that displayed a tendency to 'run in' – a cardinal fault in a gun dog of this type. Tom Evans, my mentor, disagreed with this method of bringing a runner to its senses and once when I was engaged in some activity near the rugby field that adjoined Tom's kennel he deliberately fired an acorn at my naked back. The pain was excruciating and the acorn raised a six inch bruise on my lumbar region. Tom was undismayed at my pain and simply uttered, 'Old ——'s springers were just as thin-coated as you are and the impact would have had much the same effect.' It is doubtful that Tom, – a dustbin man by trade, would ever have heard of Rousseau, but he possessed a strange inborn wisdom that made him the equal of any philosopher or behaviourist. I sorely missed him when he died.

However, if the throwing stick and its myriad variations is the subject of much debate, the use of the electric collar is an even hotter potato. The more ferocious, high-voltage affairs are now illegal in Britain, but during my spell in the USA I experienced the use of one, which I'll explain: in the late 1970s I visited a boxing promoter to research the life of Jim Jeffreys, the heavyweight fighter, and interviewed a sparring partner of the ex-world champion – an elderly fighter whose son 'bought, trained and broke' bird dogs – setters and English pointers. The trainer laid claim to being one of the most efficient trainers of bird dogs in the country and used an electric collar to produce his rapid results. I speak so often of plain old commonsense yet I so frequently fail to manifest this quality in my own day-to-day lifestyle. My curiosity about the device resulted in my wearing one such collar and the amused trainer operating the controls. The low voltage bursts produced a slight tingling in my neck and thorax; the highest voltage brought me to my knees and produced a sensation I mistook for acute angina – I was later to experience real anginal pains so I can vouch for the similarity between the sensations.

A more modern though perhaps slightly less efficacious method of controlling an offleash dog which is about to cause offence to its owner is to break the dog's concentration span and deflect his thinking towards the commands the owner is about to give. For instance, a dog about to chase a chicken will usually give ample warning of his intentions – ears will lift and the body visibly stiffen immediately prior to the attack taking place. Some trainers carry a plastic container half-filled with small stones which will rattle loudly when shaken or thrown. Others use a loud starting pistol which when fired at the appropriate moment disturbs the dog's concentration and shades of Pavlov produce a disagreeable state of fear at the moment a dog expects to experience the excitement of the chase. I have seen such methods used several times – sometimes to good effect, but frankly often to no effect whatsoever. However, a good dog-trainer is a flexible dog-trainer and one who is prepared to try any sensible methods of training an animal to achieve the desired results.

15

Dog-Training Clubs

Ogden Nash lampoons the British all too readily perhaps with his comments. 'To be an Englishman is to belong to one of the most exclusive clubs there is' but truth be told Napoleon was far from correct when he described England as a nation of shopkeepers. England, or for that matter Britain, is a nation of clubs. No country in the world boasts such a variety of clubs; there are clubs for hamster-keepers, clubs for flower-arrangers and even a club which specialises in the collection of curious epitaphs. It has been suggested that the reason why so many clubs exist in Britain is that the British are the most gregarious race in the world. In all probability it is that the British are the most competitive race in the world, and membership of any club brings about a certain degree of competitiveness amongst its members.

This fact should not stop the reader becoming a member of a dog-training club – and most towns have enthusiasts who are only too keen to run dog-training groups or clubs. Basically, dog-training clubs fall into one of four categories:

(a) Basic obedience-training clubs.
(b) Clubs which specialise in teaching dogs to compete in certain tests.
(c) Clubs which specialise in agility tests – and these tests are a recent innovation.

The standard of training expected at the various tests just mentioned extends the dogs' ability and that of the trainer though the standard expected of the dogs during these tests is seldom as precise as seen at the Kennel Club obedience tests. The Police Dog tests are the subject of some debate at the time of writing for part of the test consists of urging a dog to attack a person acting as a miscreant and to restrain or incapacitate the supposed villain. It has been argued, and in the light of recent dog attacks on children attack dogs are scarcely popular with the general public, that the ownership of attack-trained dogs should be restricted to the police force, security firms and military establishments and that the general public should not train attack dogs. It can be argued that in these troubled times when burglary, robbery with violence and murder are far from uncommon that the general public needs guard dogs that are trained to attack an intruder on command. Likewise it must be remembered that the ownership of a guard dog or an attack-trained dog is not dissimilar to the ownership of a loaded gun – and the damage even a medium-sized dog can inflict is terrifying to say the least. Furthermore, there are many laws that stipulate exactly how a trained guard dog must be kept. Under the Guard Dogs Act of 1975 (an act that was precipitated by a series of shocking attacks by ill-managed guard dogs) the use of a guard dog at any premises other than an agricultural premises or dwelling houses is not permitted unless the handler is present at all times, controls the dog at all times and a warning notice of the presence of such a dog is posted at the entrance to the premises. It should be added that if the handler is not present, the dog must be secured so that it is not at liberty to go freely about the premises. Prior to this act there was a great market for demented dogs which were cast adrift in scrap yards at night. A number of young children met with frightening accidents when they clambered fences and were attacked by these deranged animals.

Not surprisingly, the police are decidedly antipathetic to lay dog owners training dogs for the Police Dog tests, for there is no way that any club can vet unsuitable members who wish to train attack dogs as an image-maker or worse still train a dog to attack and possibly kill (and large dogs find killing a human extremely easy work) a person they may consider an enemy. A disturbed person with an attack-trained rottweiler, doberman or German shepherd dog is a terrifying prospect.

The recently devised agility tests are great fun and I would advise any person who believes a dog is demeaned or degraded by allowing itself to be trained to visit the agility tests and watch the pleasure both the handler and the dog obtain from competing in these tests. The tests consist of the dog jumping hurdles, racing through tunnels, leaping through car tyres, over seesaw-like devices and running the course against the clock. Dogs seem to love these tests and so for that matter do I. I get great pleasure watching dogs arrive at these events with excited looks on their faces and an air of expectancy that tells the observer that these tests are the highlights of these dogs' lives. It would also be hard to meet a more pleasant, ebullient band of people than one meets at these agility tests.

The specialist clubs which cater for gun dogs, sled dogs – and curiously sled dogs love sled dog races – and the newly formed lurcher training clubs which are the brain children of John O'Keeffe, Chairman of The National Lurcher Racing Club, are also highly entertaining to both dogs and dog-owners. As yet the lurcher training clubs are in an embryonic state, but it is hoped that they will become very popular.

A word of caution to end this book, however. Once winning at any event becomes the be-all and end-all of a person's life or a dog becomes unhappy competing at these events it is time for both the owner and the dog to quit. Dog-training should be fun to both the owner and the dog. When it ceases to be fun the dog trainer should seek out another hobby.

Index